W9-CFD-362

Frommer's®

P O R T A B L E

Venice

2nd Edition

**by Darwin Porter &
Danforth Prince**

Macmillan • USA

ABOUT THE AUTHORS

A native of North Carolina, **Darwin Porter** was a bureau chief for the *Miami Herald* when he was 21, and later worked in television advertising. A veteran travel writer, he wrote Frommer's first-ever guide to Italy, and he's been a frequent traveler in Italy ever since. He's joined by **Danforth Prince,** formerly of the Paris bureau of *The New York Times,* who has lived and traveled extensively in Italy. This team writes a number of best-selling Frommer guides, notably to Italy, England, France, the Caribbean, and Germany.

Thomas Worthen and **Robert Ullian,** who are responsible for the walking tours of Venice in this book, are co-authors of walking tour books to Venice. Thomas Worthen is an art historian specializing in the Italian Renaissance. Robert Ullian also authors two Frommer's guides to Israel.

MACMILLAN TRAVEL USA

A Pearson Education Macmillan Company
1633 Broadway
New York, NY 10019

Find us online at **www.frommers.com**

ISBN 0-02-862860-8
ISSN 1092-2032

Editor: Alice Fellows
With thanks to Ron Boudreau
Production Editor: Robyn Burnett
Design by Michele Laseau
Digital Cartography by Ortelius Design and Roberta Stockwell
Page Creation by Natalie Evans, David Faust, and Sean Monkhouse

SPECIAL SALES

Bulk purchases (10+ copies) of Frommer's and selected Macmillan travel guides are available to corporations, organizations, mail-order catalogs, institutions, and charities at special discounts, and can be customized to suit individual needs. For more information write to Special Sales, Macmillan General Reference, 1633 Broadway, New York, NY 10019.

Manufactured in the United States of America

Contents

List of Maps

AN INVITATION TO THE READER

In researching this book, we discovered many wonderful places—hotels, restaurants, shops, and more. We're sure you'll find others. Please tell us about them, so we can share the information with your fellow travelers in upcoming editions. If you were disappointed with a recommendation, we'd love to know that, too. Please write to:

Frommer's Portable Venice, 2nd Edition
Macmillan Travel
1633 Broadway
New York, NY 10019

AN ADDITIONAL NOTE

Please be advised that travel information is subject to change at any time—and this is especially true of prices. We therefore suggest that you write or call ahead for confirmation when making your travel plans. The authors, editors, and publisher cannot be held responsible for the experiences of readers while traveling. Your safety is important to us, however, so we encourage you to stay alert and be aware of your surroundings. Keep a close eye on cameras, purses, and wallets, all favorite targets of thieves and pickpockets.

WHAT THE SYMBOLS MEAN

✪ Frommer's Favorites

Our favorite places and experiences—outstanding for quality, value, or both.

The following abbreviations are used for credit cards:

AE	American Express	JCB	Japan Credit Bank
CB	Carte Blanche	MC	MasterCard
DC	Diners Club	V	Visa
EU	Eurocard		

FIND FROMMER'S ONLINE

Arthur Frommer's Budget Magazine Online (**www.frommers.com**) offers more than 6,000 pages of up-to-the-minute travel information—including the latest bargains and candid, personal articles updated daily by Arthur Frommer himself. No other Web site offers such comprehensive and timely coverage of the world of travel.

The Venice Experience

*O*ne rainy morning as we were leaving our hotel—a converted palazzo—a decorative stone fell from the lunette, narrowly missing us. For a second it looked as if we were candidates for a gondola funeral cortege to the island of marble tombs, San Michele. In dismay, we looked back at the owner, a woman straight from a Modigliani portrait. From the doorway, she leaned like the Tower of Pisa, mocking the buildings of her city. Throwing up her hands, she sighed, "Venezia, Venezia," then went back inside.

That woman had long ago surrendered to the inevitable decay embracing this city like the moss at the base of the pilings. Venice—La Serenissima (the Serene Republic)—is a preposterous monument to both the folly and the obstinacy of humankind. It shouldn't exist, but it does, much to the delight of thousands of visitors, gondoliers, lace makers, hoteliers, restaurateurs, and glassblowers.

Reports that Venice is sinking into the sea are exaggerated. But the enemy, which is the Adriatic, is clearly at its sea gates. When you arrive and are stunned by the architectural wonder and riches of Venice, its vivid colors of sienna, Roman gold, and ruby peach, you may think that reports of tide damage are overblown. That is, until you experience your first flood of Piazza San Marco. Then you'll see how close the sea is to sweeping over Venice.

Heroic efforts are being made to save the city. As technology advances, even more efforts will surely be expended to rescue one of the wonders of the modern world. Pollution, uncontrolled tides, and just plain old creaky age are eating away at the treasures of this fabled city of art.

Centuries ago, in an effort to flee the barbarians, Venetians left dry dock and drifted out to a flotilla of "uninhabitable" islands in the lagoon. For a long time Venice did elude foreign armies intent on burning, looting, and plundering. Of course, in time, Napoléon and his forces arrived; however, the Corsican's intent was never to destroy Venice.

Impressions

When I went to Venice—my dream became my address.

—Marcel Proust, letter to Mme Strauss (May 1906)

Foreign visitors, though, have "conquered" Venice in ways most barbarian armies did not. Some 1.2 million people visit Venice every year—that's how many visitors actually spend the night. When you count the day-trippers, the actual number may be 6 million. Few Venetians desire the presence of these day-trippers, as they tend to spend no money. Many even bring a packed lunch along. Some Venetian officials, to counter the presence of these nonspenders, have advocated that the *city* institute an admission charge.

Those who spend the night and actually dine in the restaurants are received with a much warmer embrace by the merchants, hoteliers, and restaurateurs. But even these big spenders are viewed with a certain disdain by Venetians, who'd rather have their city to themselves. Yet Venice has thrived off its visitors—everyone from Lord Byron to Ezra Pound—since the 19th century. Today, high prices have forced out many locals, who've fled across the lagoon to dreary Mestre, an industrial complex launched to help boost the regional economy and make it far less dependent on tourism. Mestre, with its factories, helps keep Venice relatively industry free, though it spews pollution across the city—hardly what the art of Venice needs.

The capital of the Veneto, Venice encompasses some 180 square miles, if Mestre, Marghera, and the islands of the lagoon are counted. Of these square miles, about 100 are water. The city is built around some 117 islands or, as is often the case, "islets." Venice is bisected by 177 canals, including its showcase artery, the palazzo-flanked Grand Canal. The islands are joined together by 400 small concrete-and-iron bridges, the most important of which are the Accademia, the Degli Scalzi, and the Rialto, all spanning the Grand Canal. Venice itself is connected to the mainland by a 3-mile bridge that crosses the Venetian lagoon to Mestre.

What will you find in Venice? Unendurable crowds; dank, dark canals and even danker, claustrophobic alleys; high, even outrageous, prices; and a certain sinister quality in the decay.

What's also here? One of the greatest—if not *the* greatest—and most spectacular cities extant ever conceived.

1 Frommer's Favorite Venice Experiences

- **Riding the Grand Canal in a Gondola:** Just before sunset, order some delectable sandwiches from Harry's Bar and a bottle of chilled Prosecco, then take someone you love on a gondola ride along the Grand Canal for the boat trip of a lifetime.
- **Sipping Cappuccino on Piazza San Marco:** Select a choice spot on one of the world's most famous and most photographed squares, order a cup of cappuccino, listen to the classical music, and absorb the special atmosphere of Venice.
- **Sunning on the Lido:** The world has seen better beaches, but few sights equal the parade of flesh and humanity of this fashionable beach on a hot summer day. Everybody from Thomas Mann's fictional von Aschenbach looking for Tadzio to a canal-swimming Byron has romped here.
- **Contemplating Giorgione's *Tempest*:** If you have time to see only one painting, make it this one at the Accademia. The artist's haunting sense of oncoming menace superimposed over a bucolic setting will stay with you long after you leave Venice.
- **Trailing Titian to the High Renaissance:** Known for his technical skill, use of brilliant color, and robust style, Tiziano Vecelli (1485–1576)—popularly known as Titian—was a master of the High Renaissance. In Venice, you can see some of this great painter's major works (those Napoléon didn't haul off to Paris) in the Accademia, Santa Maria Gloriosa dei Frari, and Santa Maria della Salute.
- **Spending a Day on Torcello:** Of all the islands in the lagoon, our favorite is Torcello, the single best day trip from Piazza San Marco. Visit, of course, to see Santa Maria Assunta, the first cathedral of Venice and home to splendid 11th- and 12th-century mosaics. But also come to explore the island, wandering around at leisure in a place time seems to have forgotten. Follow your discoveries with a lunch of cannelloni at Locanda Cipriani, and the day is yours.
- **Making a Pub Crawl in Search of *Cicchetti*:** There's no better way to escape the tourists and mingle with locals than wandering Venice's back streets in search of local color, drink, and *cicchetti* (equivalent to Spanish tapas). By the time you've made the rounds, you'll have had a great time and a full meal—everything from deep-fried mozzarella and artichoke hearts to mixed fish fries

and pizza. Finish, of course, with an ice cream at a *gelateria*. A good place to start a pub crawl is Campo San Bartolomeo near the Rialto Bridge—it's a real people's district.

- **Paying a Visit to the World's Greatest Market:** When you tire of Gothic glory and High Renaissance masterpieces, head for the Rialto Market. Here you can sample local life and see what the Venetians are going to have for dinner. It's a scene from a Canaletto painting, but unlike much of Venice, this is real. Barges, or *mototopi,* arrive throughout the day loaded with the rich produce of the Veneto and other parts. Somehow, blood-red oranges are bloodier here, fresh peas more tender and greener than elsewhere, and red radicchio redder. Of course, you'll get to meet all the sea creatures from the lagoon as well. Sample a pastry fresh from a hot oven at some little hole-in-the-wall, then cap your visit at the stall holder's favorite place, the Cantina do Mori, Calle do Mori 429, where you can belt down a glass of wine made from Tocai grapes. A tavern at this site has existed since 1462.

- **Wandering Dorsoduro:** Called the Greenwich Village of Venice, Dorsoduro attracts everybody coming to see the Peggy Guggenheim Collection or the Accademia. But few stick around to explore the district in any depth. It's worth the effort, as poet Ezra Pound would've testified. Susanna Agnelli, sister of Gianni, keeps a place here, as do many industrialists who could afford to live anywhere. Yet parts are so seedy as to look haunted. The most intriguing promenade is the Zattere, running the length of the district along the Giudecca Canal. Take a break at any watering hole; one of our favorites is the No Name Caffè, Calle Corfu 1491, between the Accademia and Campo San Barnaba.

- **Visiting the Island of the Dead:** For a Venetian, "the last gon-dola ride" is to San Michele, in the traditional funeral gondola decorated with golden angels. San Michele is a walled cemetery island shaded by massive cypresses, and there's no place quite like it. Celebrities are buried here, but so are ordinary Venetians. Time stands still in more ways than one at this cemetery. There's no more room. Today Venice has to send its dead to the main-land for burial. But poet Ezra Pound, who lived in Venice from 1959 until his death in 1972, made it just in time. It's reached by vaporetto no. 52 running from Piazza San Marco to Murano.

- **Seeing the Sun Rise on the Lagoon:** For us, there's no more enthralling experience than to get up before dawn and cross the lagoon to San Giorgio Maggiore. Architect Andrea Palladio knew exactly what he was doing when he created the church on this exact spot. The church faces Piazza San Marco and the entrance to the Grand Canal. While the tourist zillions are still asleep on the outskirts, waiting to overtake the city, you'll have Venice to yourself when the sun comes up. The architectural ensemble you can see in the first glow of dawn, the panorama in all directions as the city awakens, ranks as one of the greatest human-made spectacles on earth.

- **Experiencing Venice at 2am:** You'll truly know the meaning of the word *spectacular* when sitting at 2am on an outdoor seat on vaporetto no. 1 as it circles Venice. Only the most die-hard night owls will be on board with you. With its twinkling lights and "Titian blue" skies, Venice at this time takes on an aura unique in Europe. It's actually quiet (except for the sound of the vaporetto's motor). Perhaps a gondola, looking like a black hearse, will silently glide by. The buildings themselves take on a different mood and color, looking like ghostly mansions from another time. When you get back home, it may just be that this experience lingers longer in your memory than any other.

2

Planning a Trip to Venice

*T*his chapter contains all the nuts-and-bolts information you'll need to plan a trip to Venice, from where to get visitor information to how to get there.

1 Visitor Information & Entry Requirements

VISITOR INFORMATION

TOURIST BOARD OFFICES   For information before you go, contact the **Italian National Tourist Office**—however, Frommer's readers have repeatedly noted that the office isn't as helpful as it could be. In the United States, branches are at 630 Fifth Ave., Suite 1565, **New York,** NY 10111 (☎ **212/245-4822;** fax 212/ 586-9249); 500 N. Michigan Ave., Suite 2240, **Chicago,** IL 60611 (☎ **312/644-0990;** fax 312/644-3109); and 12400 Wilshire Blvd., Suite 550, **Los Angeles,** CA 90025 (☎ **310/820-0098;** fax 310/ 820-6357). In Canada, contact the Italian National Tourist Office at 1 Place Ville-Marie, Suite 1914, **Montréal,** Québec (☎ **514/ 866-7667;** fax 514/392-1429); and in England at 1 Princes St., **London** W1R 8AY (☎ **0171/408-1254;** fax 0171/493-6695).

THE INTERNET   Now that Europe is rushing to get on-line to keep up with the rest of the electronic world, Italy is delivering a reliable and expansive network of Web sites. However, be aware that the larger networks are often difficult to navigate, especially when you're searching for something specific.

Two good general places to start are the **European Travel Commission's** site at **www.visiteurope.com/italy** and Travel Europe's site at **www.traveleurope.it.** The **Italian National Tourist Board** sponsors **www.itwg.com,** which goes a bit further than the previous two by providing the most detailed information, including the latest rail timetables. More savvy travelers with tougher questions should seek out **www.tour-web.com,** which has everything from sports to apartment rentals to business opportunities.

Internet city guides are a good way to navigate without getting lost in the virtual countryside. You can visit Venice at **www.doge.it,**

where you'll find everything from the latest happenings to the most affordable hotel rooms.

ENTRY REQUIREMENTS

Citizens of the United States, Canada, Australia, New Zealand, and the Republic of Ireland, as well as British subjects, need only a **valid passport** to enter Italy. You don't need a visa if you aren't going to stay more than 90 days and aren't going to work there.

2 Money

CURRENCY

There are no restrictions as to how much foreign currency you can bring into Italy, though visitors should declare the amount brought in. This proves to the Italian Customs office that the currency came from outside the country, and so the same amount or less can be taken out. Italian currency taken into or out of Italy may not exceed 200,000 lire, in denominations of 50,000 lire or lower.

The basic unit of Italian currency is the **lira** (plural **lire**), abbreviated in this guide as **L.** Coins are issued in denominations of 10L, 20L, 50L, 100L, 200L, and 500L, and bills come in denominations of 1,000L, 2,000L, 5,000L, 10,000L, 50,000L, 100,000L, and 500,000L.

The **euro,** the new single European currency, became the official currency of Italy and 10 other participating countries on January 1, 1999, but not in the form of cash. The traveler may see prices displayed in euros as well as lire, and the euro can be used in noncash transactions such as credit cards. Cash will not be introduced, and the lira and other national currencies will not be replaced, until 2002.

For the best **exchange rate,** go to a bank, not to hotels or shops. Currency and traveler's checks (for which you'll receive a better rate than for cash) can be changed at the airport and some travel agencies, such as American Express and Thomas Cook. Note the rates—it sometimes pays to shop around.

TRAVELER'S CHECKS

Before leaving home, you might want to purchase traveler's checks and arrange to carry some ready cash (usually about $250, depending on your needs). In the event of theft, the value of your checks will be refunded if properly documented.

American Express (☎ **800/221-7282** in the U.S. and Canada) is one of the largest and most immediately recognized issuers of

---

The Italian Lira, the U.S. Dollar & the U.K. Pound

At this writing, $1 U.S. = approximately 1,720L (or 100L = 6¢), and this was the rate of exchange used to calculate the dollar values given throughout this book. The rate fluctuates from day to day and might not be the same when you travel to Italy.

Likewise, the ratio of the British pound to the lira fluctuates constantly. At press time, £1 = approximately 2,960L (or 100L = 3.4p).

---

traveler's checks. No commission is charged to holders of certain types of American Express cards. For questions or problems that arise outside the United States or Canada, contact any of the company's many regional representatives.

There's also **Citicorp** (☎ **800/645-6556** in the U.S. and Canada, or 813/623-1709 collect from anywhere else in the world) and **Thomas Cook** (☎ **800/223-7373** in the U.S. and Canada, or 609/987-7300 collect from anywhere else in the world), which issues MasterCard traveler's checks. **Interpayment Services** (☎ **800/ 221-2426** in the U.S. and Canada, or 212/858-8500 collect from other parts of the world), sells Visa checks that are issued by a consortium of member banks and the Thomas Cook organization.

Most Italian banks and *cambi* (currency-exchange offices) prefer traveler's checks denominated in either U.S. dollars or Swiss francs.

ATM NETWORKS

Automated-teller machines (ATMs) are becoming more and more common in Italy. If your bank card has been programmed with a personal identification number (PIN), it's likely you can use it at ATMs abroad to withdraw money from your account or as a cash advance on your credit card—just look for ATMs displaying your network's symbol (PLUS, Cirrus, whatever). But it's still smart to check with your bank to see if your PIN must be reprogrammed for usage in Italy (if you have a six-digit PIN, you'll need to get a new four-digit code). It's also a good idea to determine the frequency limits for withdrawals and cash advances on your credit card.

American Express cardholders have access to the ATMs of Banco Popolare di Milano; the transaction fee is 2% with a minimum charge of $2.50 and a maximum of $20. ATMs give a better exchange rate than banks, but some ATMs exact a service charge on

---

Beware the Acqua Alta

If you're planning to be in Venice any time from October to March, high boots can be useful. The canals flood because of a combination of the tides and the winds. If a flood is expected, a warning siren will be sounded 1 hour before crest so people can get home. The city puts out *passarelle* (boardwalks) along major routes. The *acqua alta* (high water) lasts only about 2 or 3 hours at a time.

---

every transaction. For **Cirrus** locations abroad, call ☎ **800/ 424-7787** or check out MasterCard's Web site at **www.mastercard. com/atm**. For **PLUS** usage abroad, call ☎ **800/843-7587** or visit Visa's Web site at **www.visa.com/atms**.

3 When to Go

The best months to visit are April to June and September and October. Summers are hot and muggy and the canals smelly. Winters are gray and wet but not as severe as imagined, because the natural barrier of the Lido protects central Venice from much of the fury of the Adriatic. Yet in spite of the weather, many savvy visitors prefer to visit Venice in winter, when they have the city more to themselves and can explore its treasure trove of art more leisurely.

From Easter to October, until the cold winds and rain set in, Venice is one gigantic gaudy street party. Hustlers and vendors are out in full force peddling their souvenir junk, and there's a raging circuslike atmosphere.

Venice's Average Daily Temperature (°F) & Monthly Rainfall (in.)

	Jan	Feb	Mar	Apr	May	June	July	Aug	Sept	Oct	Nov	Dec
Temp.	43	48	53	60	67	72	77	74	68	60	54	44
Rain	2.3	1.5	2.9	3.0	2.8	2.9	1.5	1.9	2.8	2.6	3.0	2.1

HOLIDAYS

Offices and shops in Italy are closed on January 1 (New Year's Day), Easter Monday, April 25 (Liberation Day), May 1 (Labor Day), August 15 (Assumption of the Virgin), November 1 (All Saints' Day), December 8 (Feast of the Immaculate Conception), December 25 (Christmas Day), and December 26 (Santo Stefano). Closings are also observed in Venice on April 25, the feast day honoring St. Mark, its patron.

VENICE CALENDAR OF EVENTS

February

✪ **Carnevale.** Carnevale is a riotous time in Venice. Theatrical presentations and masked balls cap the festivities held throughout the city and on the islands in the lagoon. The balls are by invitation, but the street events and fireworks are open to everyone. More information is available from the **Venice Tourist Office,** Azienda di Palazzetto Selva–Giardinetti Reali, Molo S. Marco (☎ **041/5-22-63-56**). The week before Ash Wednesday, the beginning of Lent.

May

• **La Sensa.** Municipal authorities conduct a pale reenactment of the once-famed ritual of the Marriage of Venice to the Sea. On the same day, the vast **La Vogalonga** ("Long Row") is held. This is an exciting 32-kilometer race to Burano and back, open to all comers. Participants reach the San Marco basin between 11am and 3pm. The Sunday after Ascension Day.

June

• **Biennale d'Arte (International Exposition of Modern Art).** One of the most famous art events in Europe takes place during alternate (odd-numbered) years. Between June and September.

July

• **Feast of Il Redentore.** This festival commemorates the end of the 1576 plague. Half of Venice picnics aboard boats and gondolas and watches spectacular fireworks. A bridge of boats spans the Giudecca Canal and connects Dorsoduro to Palladio's church of the Redentore on the island of Giudecca. Third Saturday and Sunday in July.

August

✪ **Venice International Film Festival.** Ranking after Cannes, this festival brings together stars, directors, producers, and filmmakers from all over the world. Films are shown more or less constantly between 9am and 3am in various areas of the Palazzo del Cinema on the Lido. Though good numbers of the seats are reserved for international jury members, the public can attend virtually whenever it wants, pending available seats. For information, contact the **Venice Film Festival,** c/o the Biennale office, Ca' Giustinian, Calle del Ridotto 1364A, 30124 Venezia. Call ☎ **041-521-8838** for details on how to acquire tickets or check out the Web site at **www.biennale.it**. Projected date is September 3 to 13 (usually held in August).

September
- **Regata Storica.** This is a maritime spectacular—many gondolas participate in the Grand Canal procession. However, gondolas don't race in the regatta itself. First Sunday in September.

November
- **Opera season.** During a wet and rainy season that attracts the fewest numbers of international visitors, the opera season at the theater of Malibran begins. Through mid-May.
- **Feast of the Madonna della Salute.** For approximately 24 hours, a pontoon bridge spans the Grand Canal to the great baroque church of Santa Maria della Salute for a religious procession commemorating the deliverance of Venice from the 1630–31 plague. November 21.

4 Getting There

All roads lead not necessarily to Rome but, in this case, to the docks on mainland Venice. The arrival scene at the unattractive Piazzale Roma is filled with nervous expectation; even the most veteran traveler can become confused. Whether arriving by train, bus, car, or airport limo, everyone walks to the nearby docks (less than a 5-minute walk) to select a method of transport to his or her hotel. The cheapest way is by *vaporetto* (public motorboat), the more expensive by gondola or motor launch (see "Getting Around" in chapter 3).

Warning: If your hotel is near one of the public vaporetto stops, you can sometimes struggle with your own luggage until you reach the hotel's reception area. In any event, the one time-tested piece of advice for Venice-bound travelers is that excess baggage is bad news, unless you're willing to pay dearly to have it carried for you to the docks. Porters can't accompany you and your baggage on the vaporetto.

BY PLANE

There are no direct flights from the United States to Venice; all flights go via Rome or Milan.

North American carriers that fly into Italy include **American Airlines** (☎ 800/624-6262; www.americanair.com), which flies nonstop from Chicago to Milan every evening; **TWA** (☎ 800/221-2000; www.twa.com), which offers daily nonstop flights from

New York's JFK to both Rome and Milan; and **Delta** (☎ 800/241-4141; www.delta-air.com), which flies daily from New York's JFK to both Milan and Rome. Separate flights depart every evening for both destinations. For a few months in midwinter, service to one or both of these destinations might be reduced to six flights a week. **United Airlines** (☎ 800/538-2929; www.ual.com) has service to Milan only from Dulles Airport in Washington, D.C. **US Airways** (☎ 800/428-4322; www.usairways.com) offers one flight daily to Rome out of Philadelphia (you can connect through Philly from most major U.S. cities).

Canada's second-largest airline, Calgary-based **Canadian Airlines International** (☎ 800/426-7000; www.cdnair.ca), flies every day of the week from Toronto to Rome. Two of the flights are nonstop; the others touch down en route in Montréal, depending on the schedule.

British Airways (☎ 800/AIRWAYS; www.british-airways.com), **Air France** (☎ 800/237-2747; www.airfrance.fr/en), **KLM** (☎ 800/374-7747; www.klm.nl), and **Lufthansa** (☎ 800/645-3880; www.lufthansa-usa.com) offer some attractive deals for anyone interested in combining a trip to Italy with a stopover in, say, Britain, Paris, Amsterdam, or Germany along the way.

Italy's national airline, **Alitalia** (☎ 800/223-5730 in the U.S., 514/842-8241 in Canada; www.alitalia.it/english/index.html) flies to Venice from New York via Rome or Milan. *A word to the wise:* Alitalia doesn't forbid smoking on its aircraft.

Whatever airline you fly, you'll land at Venice's **Aeroporto Marco Polo** (☎ 041/260-6111 for flight arrival and departure information) at Mestre. The **Cooperativa San Marco** (☎ 041/522-2303) operates a *motoscafo* (shuttle boat) service departing from the airport and taking visitors to Piazza San Marco in about an hour (with a stop at the Lido after about 45 minutes). The fare is 17,000L ($10). If you've got some extra lire to spend, you can arrange for a **private water taxi** by calling ☎ 041/541-5084. The cost to ride to the heart of Venice is 130,000L ($78). It's less expensive, however, to take a bus from the airport, a trip of less than 5 miles costing 5,000L ($2.90). The bus takes you across the Ponte della Libertà to the Stazione Santa Lucia, Venice's train station, at Piazzale Roma. From there you can make connections to most parts of Venice, including the Lido.

For the latest on airline Web sites, check **airlines-online.com** or **www.itn.com**.

BY TRAIN

Trains from all over Europe arrive at the **Stazione Venezia–Santa Lucia** (☎ **04178/88-088**). To get there, all trains must pass through (though not necessarily stop at) a station marked Venezia–Mestre. Don't be confused: Mestre is a charmless industrial city and the last stop on the mainland. Occasionally trains end at Mestre, in which case you'll have to catch one of the frequent 10-minute shuttle trains connecting Mestre with Venice; when booking your ticket, confirm that the train's final destination is *Stazione Santa Lucia.*

Travel time from Rome is about 5¼ hours, from Milan 3½, from Florence 4, and from Bologna 2. The best and least expensive way to get from the station to the rest of town is to take a vaporetto, which departs near the main entrance to the station.

RAIL PASSES If you'll be traveling around Italy, it makes sense to purchase a rail pass. An **Italy Rail Card** allows you to choose from 8, 15, 21, or 30 days of consecutive travel. Buy the pass in the United States, have it validated the first time you use it at any rail station in Italy, and ride as frequently as you like during the time validity. An 8-day pass costs $266 first class and $177 second class, a 15-day pass $332 first class and $168 second, a 21-day pass $386 first class and $257 second, and a 30-day pass $465 first class and $310 second.

With the Italy Rail Card and each of the other special passes offered, a **supplement** must be paid to ride on certain very rapid trains. These are designated ETR-450 trains (also known as "Pendolino" trains).

Another option is the **Italy Flexi Rail Card,** entitling holders to a predetermined number of days of travel on any rail line of Italy within a certain time period. It's ideal for passengers with set sightseeing itineraries. A pass giving 4 possible days of travel in a block of 1 month costs $209 first class and $139 second, a pass for 8 travel days over a month $293 first class and $195 second, and a pass for 12 travel days over a month $375 first class and $250 second.

You can buy these passes from travel agents or from rail agents in major cities like New York, Montréal, and Los Angeles. Eurailpasses are also available from the North American offices of CIT Travel Service, the French National Railroads, the German Federal Railroads, and the Swiss Federal Railways, or through **Rail Europe** (☎ **800/4-EURAIL**). No matter what everyone tells you,

Eurailpasses can be bought in Europe as well (at the major train stations) but are more expensive. Rail Europe can also give you information on the rail-and-drive versions of the passes.

A warning: Many irate readers have complained about train service in Italy—they've found the railroads dirty, overcrowded, unreliable, and with little regard for schedules. As you may have heard, strikes plague the country, and you never know as you board a train when it will reach your hoped-for destination. A sense of humor (and a flexible itinerary) might be your best defense against aggravation and irritating delays.

BY BUS

Buses from mainland Italy arrive in Venice at Piazzale Roma. For information about schedules, call the **ACTV office** at Piazzale Roma (☎ **041/5-28-78-86**). If you're coming from a distant city in Italy, it's better to take the train. But Venice has good bus connections with nearby cities like Padua. A one-way fare between Padua and Venice is 5,000L ($2.90). The cheapest way to reach the heart of Venice from the bus station is by vaporetto.

BY CAR

Venice has autostrada links with the rest of Italy, with direct routes from such cities as Trieste (driving time: $1^{1}/_{2}$ hours), Milan (3 hours), and Bologna (2 hours). Bologna is 94 miles southwest of Venice, Milan 165 miles west of Venice, and Trieste 97 miles east. Rome is 327 miles southwest.

If you arrive by car, there are several multitiered **parking areas** at the terminus where the roads end and the canals begin. One of the most visible is the **Garage San Marco,** Piazzale Roma (☎ **041/5-23-51-01** or 041/523-2213; fax 041/528-9969), near the vaporetto, gondola, and motor-launch docks. You'll be charged 34,000L to 46,000L ($19.70 to $26.70) per day, maybe more, depending on the size of your car. From spring to fall, this municipal car park is nearly always filled. You're more likely to find parking on the **Isola del Tronchetto** (☎ **041/5-20-75-55**), which costs 25,000L ($14.50) per day. From Tronchetto, take vaporetto no. 82 to Piazza San Marco. If you have heavy luggage, you'll need a water taxi. Parking is also available on the mainland at Mestre.

3

Getting to Know Venice

For more than 1,000 years, people have flocked to Venice because it is unlike any other city in the world. This chapter will give you information about the city layout, how to get around, and facts that you'll need to know.

1 Orientation

VISITOR INFORMATION

Visitor information is available at the **Azienda di Promozione Turistica,** Palazzetto Selva–Giardinetti Reali (Molo S. Marco) (☎ **041/5-22-63-56**). Summer hours are daily 9:30am to 6:30pm; off-season, Monday to Saturday 9:30am to 3:30pm. However, these hours aren't that consistent. Ask for a schedule of the month's special events and an updated list of museum and church hours, as these can change erratically and often. There's also a tourist office at the train station, **Stazione Venezia–Santa Lucia** (☎ **041/529-87-27**).

Anyone between 16 and 29 is eligible for a **"Rolling Venice" pass,** offering discounts in museums, certain restaurants and stores, language courses, some hotels, and even some bars. Valid for 1 year, it costs 5,000L ($2.90) and can be picked up at a special "Rolling Venice" office set up in the train station during summer.

CITY LAYOUT

MAIN ARTERIES & STREETS Venice lies 2^1/2 miles from the Italian mainland and 1^1/4 miles from the open seas of the Adriatic. It's an archipelago of some 117 islands. Most important for visitors, however, is **Piazza San Marco** (the only square in the city called *piazza*). Venice is divided into six quarters (*sestieri*): **San Marco** (the most frequented), **Santa Croce, San Polo** (officially **San Paolo**), **Castello, Cannaregio,** and **Dorsoduro.**

Many of Venice's so-called streets are actually **canals** (*rios*), somewhere around 150 in all, spanned by a total of 400 bridges. Venice's version of a main street is the **Grand Canal (Canale Grande),** which snakes through the city like an inverted S and is spanned by three bridges: the white marble **Ponte di Rialto,** the wooden **Ponte dell'Accademia,** and the stone **Ponte degli Scalzi.** The Grand Canal splits Venice into two unequal parts.

South of the section called Dorsoduro, which is south of the Grand Canal, is the **Canale della Giudecca,** a major channel separating Dorsoduro from the large island of La Guidecca. At the point where Canale della Giudecca meets the Canale di San Marco, you'll spot the little **Isola di San Giorgio Maggiore,** with a church by Palladio. The most visited islands in the lagoon, aside from the **Lido,** are **Murano, Burano,** and **Torcello.**

FINDING AN ADDRESS A maniac must've numbered Venice's buildings at least 6 centuries ago. Before you set out for a specific place, get detailed instructions and have someone mark the place on your map. Instead of depending on street numbers, try to locate the nearest cross street. Since old signs and numbers have decayed over time, it's best to look for signs posted outside rather than for a number.

A helpful hint: Every building has a street address and a mailing address, which are never the same. For example, a business at Calle delle Botteghe 3150 (Botteghe Street) will have a mailing address of San Marco 3150, since it's in the San Marco *sestiere* (district) and all buildings in an individual district are numbered continuously from 1 to 6,000. In this chapter, we give the street name first, followed by the mailing address. With this system, landmarks become important, and one of the biggest is the Grand Canal. This inverted S of a waterway splits the city in two and can actually appear on more than one side of you at once. And the sun and other navigational devices are valuable resources that can help lead you in the right direction.

Squares also take on their own Venetian character, with only San Marco actually having the piazza designation used in other Italian communities (all the other squares are *campos*). Asking directions and maintaining good humor while being thoroughly disoriented are the most important factors in getting around Venice.

STREET MAPS If you really want to tour Venice and experience that hidden, romantic trattoria on a nearly forgotten street, don't even think about using a map that doesn't detail every street and have an index on the back. The best of the lot is the **Falk map** of Venice. It details everything (well, almost), and since it's pocket-size, you can open it in the Adriatic winds without fear of it blowing away. It's sold at many news kiosks and at all bookstores.

NEIGHBORHOODS IN BRIEF

San Marco   Napoléon called it the drawing room of Europe, and it's one crowded drawing room today. The heart of Venetian life for more than 1,000 years, San Marco is where you'll find the major attractions. **Piazza San Marco (St. Mark's Square)** is dominated by the **Basilica di San Marco (St. Mark's Basilica).** Just outside the basilica is the **campanile (bell tower),** a reconstruction of the one that collapsed in 1902. Around the corner is the **Palazzo Ducale (Doge's Palace),** with its Bridge of Sighs. Piazza San Marco is also the site of some of the world's most overpriced—though famous and elegant—coffee shops, like Florian's, founded in 1720, and Quadri, which opened in 1775. (The most celebrated watering hole, however, is away from the square—Harry's Bar, founded by Giuseppe Cipriani but made famous by Hemingway.) In and around the square are some of the most convenient hotels (though not necessarily the best) and an array of expensive shops and trattorie catering to the Yankee dollar, the British pound, the German mark, or whatever.

Cannaregio   This is the gateway to Venice: It lies away from the rail station at the northwest side of the city and is the first of the six sestieri. It shelters about a third of the population of Venice, some 20,000 residents. At its heart is **Santa Lucia Station,** dating from 1955. The area also embraces the old **Jewish Ghetto,** the first on the continent. Jews began to move here at the beginning of the 16th century, when they were segregated from the rest of the city. From here, the word *ghetto* later became a generic term. Attractions in this area are the **Ca' d'Oro,** the finest example of the Venetian-Gothic style of palatial architecture; the **Chiesa della Madonna dell'Orto,** a 15th-century church known for its Tintorettos; and **Santa Maria dei Miracoli,** with a Madonna portrait supposedly able to raise the dead. Unless you're coming to view some church or palace or even the Ghetto, this area may not detain you long, as its hotels and restaurants aren't the best. Some of the cheapest lodging is along **Lista di Spagna,** immediately to the left as you exit the train station.

Castello   The shape of Venice is often likened to a fish. If so, Castello is the tail of the fish. The largest and most varied of the sestieri, Castello is home to many attractions, like the **Arsenale,** and some of the city's plushest hotels, like the **Danieli.** One of the district's most notable attractions is the Gothic **Santa Giovanni e Paolo (Zanipolo),** the Pantheon of the doges of Venice. Cutting through the sestiere is **Campo Santa Maria Formosa,** one of the largest open squares. The district's most elegant and frequented street is **Riva degli Schiavoni,** running along the Grand Canal and the site of some of the finest hotels and restaurants. It's also one of the city's favorite promenades.

San Polo   This is the heart of commercial Venice and the smallest of the sestieri, reached by crossing the **Ponte di Rialto (Rialto Bridge)** spanning the Grand Canal. The shopping here is much less expensive than in the boutiques around Piazza San Marco. One of the major attractions is the Erberia, which Casanova wrote about in his 18th-century biography. Both wholesale and retail markets still pepper this ancient site. At its center is the church of **San Giacomo di Rialto,** the oldest in the city. The district also encloses the **Scuola Grande di San Rocco,** a repository of the works of Tintoretto. **Campo San Polo** is one of the oldest and widest squares in Venice and is one of the principal venues for Carnevale. San Polo is also filled with moderately priced hotels and a large number of trattorie, many of which specialize in seafood. In general, the hotel and

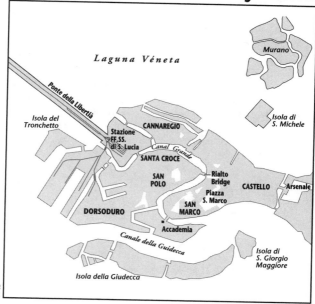

restaurant prices are cheaper here than around San Marco, but not as cheap as those around the train station in Cannaregio.

Santa Croce   This district, which takes its name from an old church that was long ago destroyed, generally follows the snakelike curve of the Grand Canal from Piazzale Roma to a point just short of the Ponte di Rialto. It's split into two rather different neighborhoods. The eastern part is in the typically Venetian style and is one of the least crowded parts of Venice, though it has some of the Grand Canal's loveliest palazzi. The western side is more industrialized and isn't very interesting to explore.

Dorsoduro   This district is compared variously to New York's Greenwich Village or London's Chelsea, though it doesn't resemble either very much. The least populated of the sestieri, it's filled with old homes and half-forgotten churches. This is the southernmost section of the historic district, and its major attraction is the **Galleria dell'Accademia.** The second most visited attraction is the **Peggy Guggenheim Foundation.** It's less trampled than the areas around the Rialto and Piazza San Marco. Its most famous church

What Would Dante Say?—Venetian Dialect

You'll have to get used to a lot of unfamiliar street designations in Venice. Even the Italians (non-Venetian ones) look befuddled when trying to decipher street names and signs (if you can even find any of the latter). Venice's colorful thousand-year history as a once-powerful maritime republic has everything to do with its local dialect, which absorbed nuances and vocabulary from the East and from the flourishing communities of foreign merchants who for centuries lived and traded in Venice. The following should give you the basics.

Ca'   The abbreviated use of the word *casa* is used for the noble palazzi, once private residences and now museums, lining the Grand Canal: Ca' d'Oro, Ca' Pesaro, and Ca' Rezzonico. There was only one palazzo: the Palazzo Ducale, the former doge's residence. However, as time went on, some great houses gradually began to be called *palazzi,* so today you'll encounter the Palazzo Grassi and the Palazzo Labia. The term *piano nobile* refers to the second or third floor of a palazzo where the principal rooms are located.

Calle   Taken from the Spanish, this is the most commonplace word for street, known as *via* or *strada* elsewhere in Italy. There

is **La Salute,** whose first stone was laid in 1631. The **Zattere,** a broad quay built after 1516, is one of the favorite promenades in Venice. Cafes and pensiones abound in the area, as do trattorie.

The Lido   This slim, sandy island (7$\frac{1}{2}$ miles long and about half a mile wide, though reaching 2$\frac{1}{2}$ miles at its broadest point) cradles the Venetian lagoon, offering protection against the Adriatic. The Lido is Italy's most fashionable bathing resort and site of the fabled **Venice Film Festival.** It was the setting for many famous books, like Thomas Mann's *Death in Venice* and Evelyn Waugh's *Brideshead Revisited.* Some of the most fashionable and expensive hotels are along the Lido Promenade. The most famous are the **Grand Hotel Excelsior** and **Grand Hotel des Bains,** but there are cheaper places as well. The best way to get around is by bike or tandem, which you can rent at Via Zara and Gran Viale.

Torcello   Lying 5$\frac{1}{2}$ miles northeast of Venice, Torcello is called "the mother of Venice," having been settled in the 9th century. It was once the most populous of the islands in the lagoon, but since are numerous variations. *Ruga,* from the French word *rue,* once meant a street flanked with stores, a designation no longer valid. A *ramo* is the branch or offshoot of a street and is often used interchangeably with calle. *Salizzada* once meant a paved street, implying that all other less important streets were just dirt alleyways. A *sotoportego* is a covered passageway.

Campo Elsewhere in Italy it's *piazza.* In Venice, the only piazza is Piazza San Marco (and its two bordering *piazzette*); all other squares are *campi* or the diminutive, *campielli.* Translated as "field" or "meadow," these were once small unpaved grazing spots for the odd chicken or cow. Almost every one of Venice's campi carries the name of the church that dominates it (or once did).

Canale There are three wide principal canals: the Canal Grande, the Canale della Giudecca, and the Canale di Cannaregio. Each of the other 160 smaller canals is called a *rio.* A *rio terrà* is a filled-in canal, wide and straight, now used as a street.

Fondamenta Referring to the foundations of the houses lining a canal, this is a walkway along the side of a rio. Promenades along the Grand Canal near Piazza San Marco and the Rialto are called *riva.*

the 18th century it has been nearly deserted. If you ever hope to find solitude in Venice, you'll find it here, following in the footsteps of Hemingway. It's visited today chiefly by those wishing to see its **Cattedrale di Torcello,** with its stunning Byzantine mosaics, and to lunch at **Locanda Cipriani.**

Burano Perched 5½ miles northeast of Venice, Burano is the most populous of the lagoon islands. In the 16th century, it produced the finest lace in Europe. Lace is still made here, but it's nothing like the product of centuries past. Inhabited since Roman times, Burano is different from either Torcello or Murano. Forget lavish palaces. The houses are often simple and small and painted in deep blues, strong reds, and striking yellows. The island is still peopled by fishers, and one of the reasons to visit is to dine in one of its trattorie, where, naturally, the specialty is fish.

Murano This island, three-quarters mile northeast of Venice, has been famed for its glassmaking since 1291. Today Murano is the most visited island in the lagoon. Once a closely guarded secret,

Murano glassmaking is now clearly visible to any tourist who wants to observe the technique on a guided tour. You can also visit a glass museum, the **Museo Vetrario di Murano,** and see two of the island's notable churches, **San Pietro Martire** and **Santi Maria e Donato.** You'll likely be on the island for lunch, and there are a number of moderately priced trattorie to be found here as well.

2 Getting Around

Since you can't hail a taxi, at least not on land, get ready to walk and walk and walk. Of course, you can break up your walks with vaporetto or boat rides. *But beware:* In summer, the overcrowding is so severe you'll often have a hard time finding room for your feet on the street.

With packed streets, more than 400 bridges, and difficult-to-board vaporetti, Venice isn't too user-friendly for those with disabilities. Nevertheless, some improvements have been made. The tourist office distributes a free map called *Veneziapertutti* (*Venice for All*), illustrating what part of Venice is accessible by the use of different color-coded references; it also outlines a list of accessible churches, monuments, gardens, public offices, hotels, and lavatories with facilities for the handicapped.

BY PUBLIC TRANSPORTATION   Much to the chagrin of the once-ubiquitous gondolier, the *vaporetti* (motorboats) of Venice provide inexpensive and frequent, if not always fast, transportation in this canal-riddled city. An *accelerato* is a vessel that makes every stop; a *diretto* makes only express stops. The average fare is 4,000L ($2.30). In summer, the vaporetti are often fiercely crowded. Pick

A Few Notes on Getting Around

Time and again while exploring, you'll think you know where you're going, only to wind up on a dead-end street or at the side of a canal with no bridge to get to the other side. Just remind yourself that Venice's physical complexity is an integral part of its charm and of the memorable experience it guarantees—getting lost is part of the fun.

Fortunately, around the city are yellow signs whose arrows direct you toward one of five major landmarks: Ferrovia (the train station), Piazzale Roma, the Rialto (Bridge), (Piazza) San Marco, and the Accademia (Bridge). You'll often find these signs grouped together, their arrows pointing off in different directions.

up a map of the system at the tourist office. There's frequent service (about every 15 minutes) daily 7am to midnight, then hourly midnight to 7am.

Line 1, the *accelerato,* is the most important for the average visitor, making all stops along the Grand Canal and continuing on to the Lido. **Line 82,** a *diretto,* also travels the Grand Canal, though it makes limited stops at Piazza San Marco, the Accademia Bridge, the Rialto Bridge, and the train station before circling Dorsoduro and crossing the lagoon to the Lido. **Line 52,** the *circolare,* is another major line, circling the perimeter of the city and crossing the lagoon to Murano on one side and the Lido on the other. **Line 12** also crosses the waves to Murano, continuing on to Burano and Torcello.

Discount Passes   You can purchase a *biglietto turistico* (tourist ticket) for 15,000L ($8.70), allowing unlimited travel all day long on any of city's boat services. A 3-day ticket is 30,000L ($17.40).

BY MOTOR LAUNCH (WATER TAXI)   It costs more than the public vaporetto, but you won't be hassled as much when you arrive with your luggage if you hire one of the city's many private motor launches, called *taxi acquei.* You may or may not have the cabin of one of these sleek vessels to yourself, since the captains fill their boats with as many passengers as the law allows before taking off. Your porter's uncanny radar will guide you to one of the inconspicuous piers where a water taxi waits.

The price of a transit by water taxi from Piazzale Roma (the road and rail terminus) to Piazza San Marco begins at 80,000L ($46.40) for up to four passengers and 100,000L ($58) for more than four. You can also call for a water taxi—try **Cooperativa San Marco** at ☎ **041/5-22-23-03.**

BY GONDOLA   If you wish to ride in a gondola, you and your gondolier have two major agreements to reach: the price of the ride and the length of the trip. If you aren't careful, you're likely to be taken on both counts. It's a common sight to see a gondolier huffing and puffing to take his passengers on a "quickie," often reducing the hour to 15 minutes. The gondolier, with his eye on his watch, is anxious to dump you and pick up the next batch of passengers. His watch almost invariably runs fast.

There *is* an accepted official rate schedule (100,000L/$58), but we've never known anyone to honor it. The actual fare depends on how well you stand up to the gondolier's attempt to get more money. Prices *begin* at 150,000L ($87) for up to 50 minutes. One

The Gondola

In *Death in Venice,* Thomas Mann wrote: "Is there anyone but must repress a secret thrill, on arriving in Venice for the first time— or returning thither after long absence—and stepping into a Venetian gondola? That singular conveyance, come down unchanged from ballad times, black as nothing else on earth except a coffin— what pictures it calls up of lawless, silent adventures in the plashing night; or even more, what visions of death itself, the bier and solemn rites and last soundless voyage!"

In the 12th century, the word *gondola* referred to the canal boats with flat bottoms traversing the canals of Venice. But it wasn't until the later 18th century that the gondola became "the taxi of Venice." The building of gondolas became a thriving and highly individualized craft, calling forth great artistry.

When gondolas got too ostentatious and the doge in 1562 thought too much money was being spent on them, he decreed that henceforth all gondolas would be painted black. Gondolas— at least the best of them—became known for their precision at maneuvering through the canals of the city.

It's estimated that in the heyday of the Renaissance, long before the age of the vaporetto, there were some 15,000 gondolas afloat in Venice—and what a sight it must have been, like a giant

gondolier confided to us that he settled for that amount in 1972. Today most gondoliers will ask at least double the official rate and reduce your time aboard to 30 to 40 minutes or even less. Prices go up after 8pm.

A word to the wise: Try to schedule your gondola ride at high tide. Otherwise you'll have an eye-level view of scum and gunk on the sides of the canals, exposed at low tide.

Two major stations at which you can rent gondolas are **Piazza San Marco** (☎ **041/520-0685**) and **Ponte di Rialto** (☎ **041/ 522-4904**).

The Grand Canal is long and snakelike and can be crossed via only three bridges, including the one at Rialto. If there's no bridge in sight, the trick in getting across is to use one of the *traghetti*— gondola-like ferries strategically placed at key points. Look for them at the end of any passage called Calle del Traghetto. Under government control, the fare is only 1,000L (60¢).

festive regatta. Nowadays there are only about 350 gondolas, mostly serving visitors wanting a ride for the thrill of it as opposed to using it as a taxi.

There are only about three gondola makers still left in Venice, though at one time there were dozens. In former days a gondola workshop might turn out 35 gondolas a year. Nowadays a gondola maker makes perhaps only four vessels, selling each craft for some $25,000 apiece, though the price could be much higher depending on elaborate ornamentation.

The art of crafting gondolas is still visible in small privately operated workshops. One that you can visit, but only if you call ahead and it's convenient for the owners and staff, is **Squèro Tramontin,** Fondamenta Ognissanti, Dorsoduro 1542 (☎ **041/523-7762;** Vaporetto: San Basilio). In sleepy Dorsoduro, it manufactures only two or three gondolas a year, painstakingly keeping alive a tradition that once dominated boatyards along the Adriatic. There'll probably be a charge of 50,000L ($30) for a 1-hour tour, and in view of the cost, you might want to skip the experience completely. But if you're absolutely, passionately devoted to the art of boatbuilding, you might find the experience worthwhile.

BY CAR

Obviously you won't need a car in Venice, but you might want one as a means of exploring such nearby cities as Padua. Most of the city's car-rental facilities lie near the rail station, in traffic-clogged Piazzale Roma. You can make arrangements at **Hertz,** Piazzale Roma 496E (☎ **800/654-3131** or 041/528-4091), open Monday to Friday 8am to 12:30am and 3 to 5:30pm and Saturday 8am to 1am. Two of its most viable competitors are **Europcar** (associated with National Car Rental in the U.S.), Piazzale Roma 496H (☎ **800/ 328-4567** or 041/523-8616), and **Avis,** Piazzale Roma 496G (☎ **800/331-2112** or 041/522-5825). They're open Monday to Friday 8:30am to 12:30pm and 2:30 to 6pm and Saturday 8:30am to 1am.

FAST FACTS: Venice

American Express   AMEX is at Salizzada San Moisè, San Marco 1471 (☎ **041/5-20-08-44**). City tours and mail handling can be obtained here. May to October, hours are Monday to Saturday 8am to 8pm for currency exchange and 9am to 5:30pm for all other transactions; off-season hours are Monday to Friday 9am to 5:30pm and Saturday 9am to 12:30pm.

Business Hours   Regular business hours for offices and shops are generally Monday to Friday 9am to 1pm and 3:30 to 7 or 7:30pm. July to September, offices may not open in the afternoon until 4 or 4:30pm. Banks in Venice are open Monday to Friday 8:30am to 1:30 or 2pm and 3 to 4pm; they're closed all day Saturday, Sunday, and national holidays.

Consulates   There's no **U.S. Consulate** in Venice; the closest is in Milan, at Via Principe Amedeo 2 (☎ **02/290-351**). The **U.K. Consulate** is at Dorsoduro 1051, at the foot of the Accademia Bridge (☎ **041/522-7207**), open Monday to Friday 10am to noon and 2 to 3pm. The nearest **Canadian** and **Australian** consulates are in Milan as well, so we suggest going to the U.K. consulate.

Currency Exchange   There are many banks in Venice where you can exchange money. You might try the Banco Commerciale Italiana, Via XXII Marzo, San Marco 2188 (☎ **041/529-6811**), or Banco San Marco, Calle Larga S. Marco, San Marco 383 (☎ **041/529-3711**).

Customs   Upon leaving Italy, citizens of the United States who've been outside the country for 48 hours or more are allowed to bring back $400 worth of merchandise duty free—that is, if they haven't claimed a similar exemption in the past 30 days. If you make purchases in Italy, it's important to keep your receipts.

Dentists   Your best bet is to have your hotel call and set up an appointment with an English-speaking dentist. The American Express office and the U.K. Consulate also have a list.

Doctors   See "Hospitals," below. The suggestion given for a dentist in Venice (above) also pertains to English-speaking doctors.

Drugstores   If you need a drugstore in the middle of the night, call ☎ **192** for information about which one is open. Pharmacies take turns staying open late. Well recommended is the centrally located International Pharmacy, Via XXII Marzo, San Marco 2067 (☎ **041/5-22-23-11**).

Emergencies   Call ☎ **113** for police, ☎ **118** for an ambulance, and ☎ **115** to report a fire.

Hospitals   Get in touch with the Civili Riuniti di Venezia, Campo Santi Giovanni e Paolo (☎ **041/5-29-41-11**), which is staffed with English-speaking doctors 24 hours a day.

Luggage Storage & Lockers   These services are available at the main rail station, Stazione di Santa Lucia, at Piazzale Roma (☎ **041/71-55-55**). The cost is 5,000L ($2.90) per package.

Newspapers & Magazines   The *International Herald Tribune* and *USA Today* are sold at most newsstands and in many first-class and deluxe hotels, as are the European editions (in English) of *Time* and *Newsweek.*

Post Office   The main post office is at Salizzada Fontego dei Tedeschi, San Marco 5554 (☎ **041/271-7111**), in the vicinity of the Rialto Bridge. It's open Monday to Saturday 8:15am to 7pm.

Rest Rooms   These are available at Piazzale Roma and various other places in Venice but aren't as plentiful as they should be. Often you'll have to rely on the facilities of a cafe, though you should purchase something—perhaps a light coffee—as in theory, commercial establishments reserve their toilets for customers only. Most museums and galleries have public toilets. You can also use the public toilets at the Albergo Diurno, on Via Ascensione, just behind Piazza San Marco. Remember, *Signori* means men and *Signore* women.

Safety   The curse of Venice is the pickpocket artist. Violent crime is rare. But because of the overcrowding in vaporetti and even on the small narrow streets, it's easy to pick pockets. Purse snatchings are commonplace as well. A purse snatcher can dart out of nowhere, grab a purse, and in seconds, disappear down some narrow dark alleyway. Keep your valuables locked in a safe in your hotel, if one is provided.

Taxes   A 19% value-added tax (called IVA in Italy) is added to the price of all consumer goods and products and most services, such as those in hotels and restaurants. For information on how to get an IVA tax refund, see "Tax Refunds" in chapter 8.

Telegrams, Telex & Fax   The post office maintains a telegram and fax service 24 hours a day. You can also call ITALCABLE at ☎ **170** if you wish to send an international telegram; otherwise, call ☎ 186. Chances are your hotel will send or receive a telex or fax for you.

Telephone   The country code for Italy is **39.** The city code for Venice is **041;** use this code when you're calling from outside Italy, when you're calling from within Italy but not in Venice, and even when you're calling within Venice. To call Venice from the United States, you would dial 011 + 39 + 041 + the number.

A public telephone is always near at hand in Venice, especially if you're near a bar. Local calls cost 200L (10¢). You can use 100L, 200L, or 500L coins. Most phones accept a multiple-use phone card called CartaSIP, which you can buy at all *tabacchi* (tobacco shops) and bars in increments of 2,000L, 5,000L, 10,000L, or 20,000L. To use this card, insert it into the slot in the phone and then dial. A digital display will keep track of how many lire you use up. The card is good until it runs out of lire, so don't forget to take it with you when you hang up.

Thanks to ITALCABLE, international calls to the United States and Canada can be dialed directly. Dial **00** (double zero, the international code from Italy), then the country code (1 for the United States and Canada), the area code, and the number you're calling. Calls dialed directly are billed on the basis of the call's duration only. A reduced rate is applied from 11pm to 8am Monday to Saturday and all day Sunday.

If you wish to make a collect call from a pay phone, simply deposit 200L (don't worry, you get it back when you're done) and dial **170,** and an ITALCABLE operator will come on and will speak English.

For calling-card calls, drop in the refundable 200L, then dial the appropriate number for your card's company to be connected with an operator in the United States: 172-1011 for AT&T, 172-1022 for MCI, and 172-1877 for Sprint.

If you make a long-distance call from a public telephone, there's no surcharge. However, hotels have been known to double or triple the cost of the call, so be duly warned.

Time   In terms of standard time zones, Italy is 6 hours ahead of eastern standard time in the United States. Daylight saving time goes into effect in Italy each year from the beginning of April to the end of September.

Tipping   In hotels, the service charge of 15% to 19% is already added to a bill. In addition, it's customary to tip the chambermaid 1,000L (60¢) per day, the doorman (for calling a cab) 1,000L (60¢), and the bellhop or porter 3,000L to 5,000L ($1.75 to $2.90) per bag. A concierge expects about 15% of his or her bill, as well as tips for extra services, which could include help with long-distance calls. In expensive hotels these lira amounts are often doubled.

In restaurants, 15% is added to your bill to cover most charges. An additional tip for good service is almost always expected. It's customary in certain fashionable restaurants to leave an additional 10%, which, combined with the assessed service charge, is a very high tip indeed. The sommelier expects 10% of the cost of the wine. Checkroom attendants now expect 1,500L (85¢), though in simple places Italians still hand washroom attendants 200L to 300L (10¢ to 15¢), more in deluxe and first-class establishments. Restaurants are required by law to give customers official receipts.

In cafes and bars, tip 15% of the bill and give a theater usher 1,500L (85¢). Taxi drivers expect at least 15% of the fare.

Transit Information   For flights, call ☎ **041/2-60-61-11;** for rail information, call ☎ **0478/88-088** toll free in Italy only; and for bus schedules, call ☎ **041/5-28-78-86.**

4

Accommodations

Venice has some of the most expensive hotels in the world, like the Gritti Palace and the Cipriani. But there are also dozens of unheralded moderately priced places, often on hard-to-find narrow streets. Venice has never been known, however, as an inexpensive destination.

Because of age and lack of uniformity, Venice's hotels offer widely varying rooms. For example, it's entirely possible to stay in a hotel generally considered "expensive" while paying only a "moderate" rate—if you'll settle for a less desirable room. Many "inexpensive" hotels and boarding houses have two or three rooms in the "expensive" category. Usually these accommodations are more spacious and open onto a view. Also, if an elevator is essential for you, always inquire in advance when booking a room.

The cheapest way to visit Venice is to book into a *locanda* (small inn), rated below the *pensioni* (boarding houses). Standards are highly variable in these places, many of which are dank, dusty, and dark. The rooms even in many second- or first-class hotels are often cramped, as space has always been a problem in Venice. It's estimated that in this "City of Light," at least half the rooms in any category are dark, so be duly warned. Those with lots of light opening onto the Grand Canal carry a hefty price tag.

The most difficult times to find rooms are during Carnevale (February), Easter, and from June to September. Because of the tight hotel situation, it's advisable to make reservations as far in advance as possible. After those peak times, you can virtually have your pick of rooms. Most hotels, if you ask at the reception desk, will grant you a 10% to 15% discount November to March 15. But getting this discount may require a little negotiation. A few hotels close in January if there's no prospect of business.

If you want to avoid the crowds, consider staying in San Polo or Dorsoduro, which aren't as touristy, where you stand a chance of experiencing the "real" Venice. Connoisseurs of Venice often prefer Dorsoduro because the presence of the university means there are lots of informal cafes and inexpensive trattorie. Most visitors, however, prefer the hotels in and around Piazza San Marco, though these tend to be expensive and the district is virtually overrun. Hotels around the more commercial Ponte di Rialto are often far less expensive but also less desirable. In the Castello district, hotel prices vary according to their proximity to Piazza San Marco.

Should you arrive without a reservation, go to one of the **AVA (Hotel Association) reservations booths** throughout the area at the train station, the municipal parking garage at Piazzale Roma, the airport, and the information point on the mainland where the highway comes to an end. The main office is at Piazzale Roma (☎ **041/ 522-8640**). To secure a room you're required to post a deposit that's then rebated on your hotel bill. Depending on the hotel classification, deposits are 20,000L to 90,000L ($12 to $52) per person. All hotel booths are open daily 9am to 8 or 9pm.

1   Best Bets

- **Best Historic Hotel:** Still the most prestigious address, the **Gritti Palace,** Campo Santa Maria del Giglio, San Maro 2467 (☎ **800/ 325-3535** or 041/79-46-11), remains quintessential Venice. Behind its chaste Gothic facade on the Grand Canal, it was the home of 15th-century doge Andrea Gritti. But since it became a hotel in 1948, it's been celebrity haunted—everyone from Winston Churchill to Elizabeth II. Even most of the furnishings are worthy of a museum.

- **Best for a Romantic Getaway:** A sybaritic retreat, the **Hotel Cipriani,** Isola della Giudecca 10 (☎ **800/992-5055** or 041/ 5-20-77-44), was founded in 1958 by Giuseppe Cipriani, who became the world's most famous "bartender" with his creation of Harry's Bar on the Grand Canal. Just a boat ride from Piazza San Marco, this sumptuous hotel attracts both honeymooners and off-the-record weekenders. Guests are pampered with private butler service, but the discreet staff knows when to let you alone—that is, when you think more than two's a crowd.

- **Best Trendy Hotel:** If you're rich, famous, or stop traffic when you don a bikini (male or female), then the place to see and be seen is the **Excelsior Palace,** Lungomare Marconi 41 (☎ **800/ 325-3535** or 041/5-26-02-01), on the Venetian Lido. It was fashionable way back in the early 1900s, and, if anything, it's even more fashionable today—especially when it becomes the unofficial headquarters of the Venice Film Festival.

- **Best Hotel Lobby for Pretending You're Rich:** They weren't always rich, but the crowned heads of Europe, joined by political and literary giants, have long enjoyed the lobby of the **Danieli Royal Excelsior,** Riva degli Schiavoni, Castello 4196 (☎ 800/ 325-3535 or 041/5-22-64-80). The lobby is the most palatial in Venice, as Charles Dickens, Honoré de Balzac, Richard Wagner, Gabrielle D'Annunzio, and George Sand would surely have agreed. Drop in for tea in the afternoon at this chic rendezvous, then sit back and sip your "cuppa" under the Murano chandeliers while surveying a field of marble columns.

- **Best for Families:** If you don't want to break the bank and are in Venice with the brood, head for the Lido and seek lodgings at the **Hotel Belvedere,** Piazzale Santa Maria Elisabetta 4 (☎ 041/ 5-26-57-73). Still run by the same family since 1857, it has long been receiving parents with children from all over the world. Recently restored and modernized, it has rooms with a view of St. Mark lagoon, plus a good moderately priced restaurant.

- **Best Moderately Priced Hotel:** Hidden away in the Santa Croce district, the **Hotel San Cassiano Ca' Favretto,** Calle della Rosa 2232 (☎ 041/5-24-17-68), was once the studio of 19th-century painter Giacomo Favretto. As you take your breakfast, you can enjoy views of the lacy facade of the Ca' d'Oro, Venice's most beautiful building. Antiques or high-quality reproductions fill the rooms, and everything is comfortably old-fashioned—all at a good price. You'll also avoid the crowded area around St. Mark's if you anchor here.

- **Best Budget Hotel:** The most patrician of pensioni, the **Pensione Accademia,** Fondamenta Bollani, Dorsoduro 1058 (☎ 041/5-23-78-46) was the setting for Katharine Hepburn's residence in the film *Summertime.* This 17th-century villa is swaddled in a tranquil garden off the Grand Canal and near the Accademia. Personalized service and a friendly ambience are the hallmarks of this longtime favorite.

- **Best Canalside Inn:** In the Dorsoduro area (the Greenwich Village of Venice), the **Locanda Montin,** Fondamenta di Borgo 1147 (☎ 041/5-22-71-51), may be short on private bathrooms, but it's long on charm. Four rooms (and these go first) have small terraces lined with geraniums, opening onto views of the canal. Though it's only a fourth-class hotel, many luminaries have made their way here, including Pres. Jimmy Carter. The most authentic Venetian cuisine is served in the restaurant downstairs.

- **Best Service:** The Cipriani, Gritti, and Danieli may grab the glitter and glamour, but for quality service and warm hospitality, none of them equals the care and charm provided by the staff at the **Quattro Fontane,** Via Quattro Fontane 16 (☎ **041/5-26-02-27**), on the Lido, transformed from a 19th-century villa. Its service is most exemplary at afternoon tea, served in a tranquil garden. You get the feeling you're the guest in an elegant private home. Most of the staff has been here for a quarter of a century.

- **Best Location:** The only hotel with rooms overlooking Piazza San Marco, the **Hotel Concordia,** Calle Larga, San Marco 367 (☎ **041/5-20-68-66**), is now moving toward its second century. It's hardly the grandest hotel in the St. Mark's area, but the setting and view more than compensate. Imagine waking up and looking out your window onto what has been called "the drawing room of Europe."

- **Best Views:** Though there are challengers, like the Gritti Palace, few hotels can equal the view of the Grand Canal offered from the rooms of the **Hotel Monaco & Grand Canal,** Calle Vallaresso, San Marco 1325 (☎ **041/5-20-02-11**). Harry's Bar is right across the way, and Piazza San Marco is only 2 blocks away. But even those stellar attractions are forgotten when you see the view outside your window.

2 San Marco

VERY EXPENSIVE

✪ **Gritti Palace.** Campo Santa Maria del Giglio, San Marco 2467, 30124 Venezia. ☎ **800/325-3535** in the U.S. and Canada, or 041/79-46-11. Fax 041/5-20-09-42. www.luxurycollection.com. 99 units. A/C MINIBAR TV TEL. 847,000L–1,100,000L ($491.25–$638) double; from 2,090,000L ($1,212.20) suite. AE, DC, MC, V. Vaporetto: Santa Maria del Giglio.

The Gritti, in a stately setting on the Grand Canal, is the renovated palazzo of the 15th-century doge Andrea Gritti. Even after its takeover by Sheraton ITT, it's still a bit starchy, but in terms of prestige only the Cipriani tops it. The place has a bit of a museum aura (some of the original furnishings are roped off, for example). For Hemingway it was his "home in Venice," and for years it has drawn royal, political, literary, and theatrical figures. The range and variety of rooms seem almost limitless, from elaborate suites to relatively small singles. But in every case, the glamour is evident. For a splurge, ask for Hemingway's old suite or the Doge Suite, once occupied by Somerset Maugham.

Dining: The Ristorante Club del Doge is among the best in Venice but also egregiously priced.

Venice Accommodations

Alloggi ai do Mori **14**
American Hotel **26**
Bonvecchiati **7**
Boston Hotel **15**
Danieli Royal Excelsior **31**
Doni Pensione **29**
Gritti Palace **21**
Hotel Abbazia **1**
Hotel Bernardi-Semenzato **2**
Hotel Bisanzio **26**
Hotel Campiello **27**
Hotel Carpaccio **6**
Hotel Casanova **18**
Hotel Cavaletto e Doge Orseolo **16**
Hotel Cipriani **32**
Hotel Concordia **13**
Hotel Do Pozzi **20**
Hotel Europa & Regina **22**
Hotel Geremia **1**
Hotel Giorgione **3**
Hotel la Fenice et des Artistes **18**
Hotel Luna Baglioni **24**
Hotel Marconi **4**
Hotel Monaco & Grand Canal **23**
Hotel Montecarlo **12**
Hotel Piave **8**
Hotel Rialto **5**
Hotel Riva **10**
Hotel San Cassiano Ca' Favretto **1**
Hotel Scandinavia **9**
La Calcina **33**
La Residenza **25**
Locanda Montin **33**
Locanda Remedio **11**
Locando Sturion **5**
Londra Palace **28**
Pensione Accademia **34**
Saturnia-International **19**
Savoia & Jolanda **30**

Legend
Church ⛪

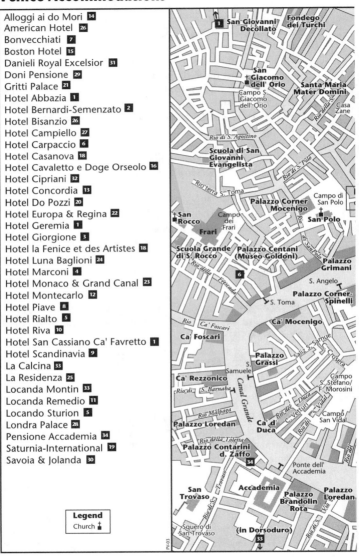

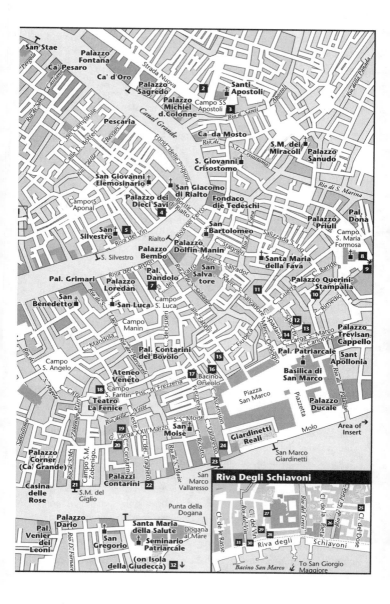

San'Stae

Palazzo
Fontana
Ca' Pesaro

Ca' d'Oro

Palazzo
Sagredo

Palazzo
Michiel
d.Colonne

2

Santi
Apostoli

Campo SS
Apostoli

3

Strada Nuova

Canal Grande

Pescaria

Ca' da Mosto

Rio di

S. Giovanni
Crisostomo

S.M. dei
Miracoli

Palazzo
Sanudo

San Giovanni
Elemosinario †

San Giacomo
di Rialto

Fondaco
die Tedeschi

Rio di S. Marina

Palazzo dei
Dieci Savi **4**

San †
Silvestro **5**

San
†Bartolomeo

Palazzo
Priuli

Pal.
Donà

Campo
S. Maria
Formosa

Palazzo
Bembo

Palazzo
Dolfin Manin

Santa Maria
della Fava

8

9

Pal. Grimani

Palazzo
Loredan

Pal.
Dandolo **7**

San
Salva-
tore

Palazzo Querini-
Stampalia

10

San
Benedetto ■

■ San Luca

Campo
S. Luca

11

12

13

Palazzo
Trevisan-
Cappello

Campo
Manin

14

Largo S. Marco

Pal. Contarini
del Bovolo

15

Pal. Patriarcale

Sant
Apollonia

Campo
S. Angelo

Ateneo
Veneto

16

17 Bacino
Orseolo

Basilica di
San Marco

Teatro
La Fenice **18**

Campo
S. Fantin

Piazza
San Marco

Palazzo
Ducale

19

Largo XXII Marzo

San
Moisè

Piazzetta

Palazzo
Corner
(Ca' Grande)

20

24

Giardinetti
Reali

Molo

Area of
Insert →

Palazzi
Contarini **22**

23

San Marco
Giardinetti

21

S.M. del
Giglio

San Marco
Vallaresso

Bacino San Marco

Casina
delle
Rose

Riva Degli Schiavoni

Palazzo
Dario

Punta della
Dogana

27

25

Pal.
Venier
dei
Leoni

San
Gregorio

Santa Maria
della Salute

Dogana
al Mare

26

29

Seminario
Patriarcale

31 **30**

Riva degli

Schiavoni

(on Isola
della Giudecca) **32** ↓

To San Giorgio
Maggiore

35

Amenities: 24-hour room service, baby-sitting, laundry, valet; use of the Hotel Excelsior's facilities on the Lido.

Hotel Europa & Regina. Via XXII Marzo, San Marco 2159, 30124 Venezia. ☎ **800/221-2340** in the U.S. and Canada, or 041/5-20-04-77. Fax 041/5-23-30-43. www.luxurycollection.com. 185 units. A/C MINIBAR TV TEL. 737,000L–935,000L ($427.45–$542.30) double. Rates include breakfast. AE, DC, MC, V. Vaporetto: San Marco.

A longtime favorite on the Grand Canal, the Europa & Regina can be reached by motorboat at its canal-side entry or through a court-yard on Via XXII Marzo. In 1997, a $25-million renovation was completed to return it to five-star status. The hotel was formed by combining two Venetian palaces, both facing the Grand Canal and La Salute, with a restaurant terrace and a cafe terrace between. The guest rooms are in a neobaroque or Empire style, and the most expensive are those facing the Grand Canal. Some upper-floor rooms offer terraces with panoramic views, and many accommodations have fireplaces and small balconies.

Dining/Diversions: An American-style piano bar becomes an afternoon tearoom, and the hotel restaurant spills out on a Grand Canal terrace. The food is much better at the Gritti, but you do get some good-tasting regional dishes.

Amenities: 24-hour room service, concierge, conference rooms, baby-sitting, laundry.

Hotel Luna Baglioni. Calle Vallaresso, San Marco 1243, 30124 Venezia. ☎ **041/5-28-98-40.** Fax 041/5-28-71-60. E-mail: luna.venezia@ palacehotels. it. 125 units. A/C MINIBAR TV TEL. 350,000L–720,000L ($203–$417.60) double; 950,000L–1,800,000L ($551–$1,044) suite. Rates include buffet breakfast. AE, DC, MC, V. Vaporetto: San Marco.

The Luna is Venice's oldest hotel but was long ago modernized in an international style. Even though it retains traces of its gracefully Napoleonic look, it lacks the sumptuous mottled patina of the Danieli or the Gritti. Founded in 1474 as a monastery by the Congrega di Fratti della Luna, it took in traveling pilgrims on their way through Venice. Rooms on the fourth floor and above look over the Grand Canal, and most of them have high ceilings, renovated interiors, and marble and parquet floors. The rooms are luxurious with big chandeliers and fabric-covered walls; a few feature small balustraded balconies. Floral bouquets are in the halls of the upper floors, which can be reached by elevator or by a wide marble staircase.

Dining: The hotel serves a refined Venetian and international cuisine in its Ristorante Canova. The Venetian-style bar overlooking a canal opposite the ducal gardens is a cozy retreat.

Amenities: Room service (7am to midnight), baby-sitting, laundry, valet.

✪ **Hotel Monaco & Grand Canal.** Calle Vallaresso, San Marco 1325, 30124 Venezia. ☎ **041/5-20-02-11.** Fax 041/5-20-05-01. 70 units. A/C MINIBAR TV TEL. 590,000L–680,000L ($342.20–$394.40) double; 790,000–990,000L ($458.20–$574.20) suite. Rates include breakfast. AE, DC, MC, V. Vaporetto: San Marco.

The intimate and refined Monaco & Grand Canal captures the essence of Venice with its panoramic Grand Canal view. It's in the same league as the Luna Baglioni (above) but a second-tier choice when stacked up against the Cipriani, Danieli, and Gritti. Harry's Bar is right across the way and Piazza San Marco only 2 blocks away. This five-star hotel is a favorite with discriminating Italians, particularly in fall and winter. It was the choice place of Simone de Beauvoir and Jean-Paul Sartre; more recently, Prince Rainier stayed here. These savvy guests took the upper rooms to escape the noise from the nearby vaporetto terminal. The guest rooms are a medley of styles, including painted furniture and provincial styling. Their appointments are rich and lush, with Murano chandeliers, silk wall coverings, antique desks, and white tiled bathrooms. There are no balconies.

Dining: The hotel harbors one of the city's leading restaurants, named for the Grand Canal, where you can enjoy high-quality Venetian specialties as well as impeccable service and a panorama. In season, meals are also served on the terrace along the canal.

Amenities: 24-hour room service, concierge, baby-sitting, laundry, valet.

EXPENSIVE

Hotel Casanova. Frezzeria, San Marco 1284, 30124 Venezia. ☎ **041/520-6855.** Fax 041/520-6413. 49 units. A/C MINIBAR TV TEL. 340,000L ($197.20) double; 420,000L ($243.60) triple; 370,000L ($214.60) suite. Rates include breakfast. AE, DC, MC, V. Vaporetto: San Marco.

This former home is a few steps from Piazza San Marco. Though the name Casanova sounds romantic, the hotel doesn't have a lot of character; it does, however, contain a collection of church art and benches from old monasteries (sitting on flagstone floors near oil portraits). The modernized guest rooms are for the most part devoid of charm yet generally well maintained and comfortable. The accommodations vary considerably in size—some are quite small. The most intriguing units are found on the top floor, with exposed brick walls and sloping beam ceilings.

Dining: Breakfast is the only meal served, but there are many dining choices outside your door.

Amenities: Concierge, room service (drinks only, no food; 7am to 10pm), laundry, newspaper delivery on request, twice-daily maid service.

Hotel Cavaletto e Doge Orseolo. Calle del Cavalletto, San Marco 1107, 30124 Venezia. ☎ **041/5-20-09-55.** Fax 041/5-23-81-84. E-mail: cavaletto@tiw.it. 96 units. A/C MINIBAR TV. 320,000L–490,000L ($185.60–$284.20) double. Rates include breakfast. AE, DC, MC, V. Vaporetto: San Marco.

This hotel, with the accumulated patina of an 800-year history, occupies a prime position on a narrow cobblestone street a few paces from St. Mark's Square. The hotel was created when three buildings were unified into one in the early 1900s. In the 1100s, the oldest of the three was the home of Doge Orseolo. In some ways, the setting is far more romantic than the hotel, which has none of the refined service of the properties previously recommended. Today the Cavaletto is best viewed from its sinuously curved rear, where a flotilla of gondolas is moored in a stone-sided harbor, one of only two such basins in Venice. Each of the hotel's guest rooms is outfitted with glass chandeliers from nearby Murano, hardwood floors, and elegant Italian-inspired furniture. Many have views of canals, but these tend to be noisy.

Dining/Diversions: The hotel has a big-windowed restaurant, with reflected sun from the lagoon dappling the high ceiling. Only breakfast is offered here, but dinner is served in the two other restaurants in adjacent buildings. There's also a kind of *dolce vita* bar where a relaxing cocktail might be the perfect end to a day.

Amenities: 24-hour room service, concierge, baby-sitting, laundry.

✪ **Hotel Concordia.** Calle Larga, San Marco 367, 30124 Venezia. ☎ **041/5-20-68-66.** Fax 041/5-20-67-75. www.italyhotel.com/home/venezia/concordia/concordia.html. E-mail: veniceitaly@hotelconcordia.com. 58 units. A/C MINIBAR TV TEL. 310,000L–590,000L ($179.80–$342.20) double. Rates include buffet breakfast. AE, DC, MC, V. Vaporetto: San Marco.

The four-star Concordia, in a russet-colored building with stone-trimmed windows, is the only hotel with rooms overlooking St. Mark's Square. A series of gold-plated marble steps takes you to the lobby, where you'll find a comfortable bar area, good service, and elevators to whisk you to the labyrinthine halls. All guest rooms are decorated in a Venetian antique style and contain, among other amenities, an electronic safe and a hair dryer.

Dining: Breakfast is the only meal served, but light meals and Italian snacks are available in the bar.

Amenities: 24-hour room service, baby-sitting, laundry/valet.

Hotel Saturnia International. Via XXII Marzo, San Marco 2399, 30124 Venezia. ☎ **041/5-20-83-77.** Fax 041/5-20-71-31. www.italyhotel.com/venezia/saturnia. E-mail: saturnia@doge.it. 95 units. A/C MINIBAR TV TEL. 336,000L–630,000L ($194.90–$365.40) double. Rates include breakfast. AE, DC, MC, V. Vaporetto: San Marco.

The Saturnia International was skillfully created from a 14th-century palazzo near Piazza San Marco. You're surrounded by richly embellished beauty here—a grand hallway with a wooden staircase, heavy iron chandeliers, fine paintings, and beamed ceilings. The individually styled guest rooms are spacious and furnished with chandeliers, Venetian antiques, tapestry rugs, gilt mirrors, and ornately carved ceilings. Many overlook the hotel's quiet courtyard.

Dining: For details about the hotel's restaurant, La Caravella, see chapter 5, "Dining."

Amenities: 24-hour room service, baby-sitting, laundry, valet.

Hotel Scandinavia. Campo Santa Maria Formosa, Castello 5240, 30122 Venezia. ☎ **041/5-22-35-07.** Fax 041/5-23-52-32. 39 units. A/C MINIBAR TV TEL. 370,000L–500,000L ($214.60–$290) double. Rates include breakfast. AE, MC, V. Vaporetto: San Zaccaria.

This hotel isn't in San Marco—it's in neighboring Castello—but it has a convenient location not far from Piazza San Marco, so we've placed it in this section. A radical 1992 overhaul added a third star to this hotel's rating. The entrance is set behind a dark-pink facade just off one of the most colorful squares in Venice. The public rooms are filled with copies of 18th-century Italian chairs, Venetian-glass chandeliers, and a re-created rococo decor. The guest rooms are decorated in the Venetian style, but with modern comforts. There's also a bar and 24-hour room service (for drinks). A lobby lounge overlooks Campo Santa Maria Formosa.

MODERATE

Hotel Bonvecchiati. Calle Goldoni, San Marco 4488, 30124 Venezia. ☎ **041/5-28-50-17.** Fax 041/5-28-52-30. www.hotelinvenice.it. 86 units. TEL. 230,000L–310,000L ($133.40–$179.80) double. Rates include breakfast. AE, DC, MC, V. Vaporetto: San Marco or Rialto.

The Bonvecchiati, which looks a lot like a private villa, has seen better days but is still a viable choice because of it's near San Marco.

With the closing of its restaurant and terrace, it seems to be running only at half steam and is indifferently staffed. Breakfast is served in a small dining room off the lobby, and maintenance isn't always the best. The rooms, for the most part, are traditionally appointed and contain a number of amenities, like private safes and minibars. Air-conditioning is available on request.

Hotel do Pozzi. Corte do Pozzi, San Marco 2373, 30124 Venezia. ☎ **041/5-20-78-55.** Fax 041/5-22-94-13. 35 units. MINIBAR TV TEL. 260,000L ($150.80) double. Rates include breakfast. AE, DC, MC, V. Vaporetto: Santa Maria del Griglio.

Small, modernized, and just a short stroll from the Grand Canal and Piazza San Marco, this place is more like a country tavern than a hotel. Its original structure is 200 years old, opening onto a paved courtyard with potted greenery. You can arrive via water taxi, boat, gondola, or vaporetto. The sitting and dining rooms are furnished with antiques (and near antiques) intermixed with utilitarian modern decor. Baths have been added, and a major refurbishing has given everything a fresh touch. Laundry and baby-sitting are available.

Hotel La Fenice et des Artistes. Campiello de La Fenice, San Marco 1936, 30124 Venezia. ☎ **041/5-23-23-33.** Fax 041/5-20-37-21. 69 units. TV TEL. 310,000L–340,000L ($179.80–$197.20) double; 390,000L–440,000L ($226.20–$255.20) suite. Rates include breakfast. AE, DC, MC, V. Vaporetto: San Marco.

This hotel offers widely varying accommodations in two connected buildings, each at least 100 years old. One is rather romantic, though a bit timeworn, with an impressive staircase leading to the overly decorated rooms (one was once described as "straight out of the last act of *La Traviata*, enhanced by small gardens and terraces"). Your satin-lined room may have an inlaid desk and a wardrobe painted in the Venetian manner to match a baroque bed frame. The carpets might be thin, however, and the fabrics aging. The rooms in the other building are far less glamorous, with modern sterile furniture. All but about three of the rooms are air-conditioned.

Hotel Montecarlo. Calle dei Specchieri, San Marco 463, 30124 Venezia. ☎ **800/528-1234** or 041/5-20-71-44. Fax 041/5-20-77-89. www.italyhotel.com/venezia/montecarlo or www.bestwestern.com. E-mail: mocarlo@doge.it. 48 units. A/C TV TEL. 180,000L–400,000L ($115.20–$256) double. Rates include breakfast. AE, DC, MC, V. Vaporetto: San Marco.

Just a 2-minute walk from Piazza San Marco, this hotel opened some years ago in a 17th-century building but was recently renovated to include modern tile bathrooms. The upper halls are lined with paintings by Venetian artists. The double rooms are comfortably proportioned and decorated with Venetian-style furniture and Venetian-glass chandeliers. The hotel's restaurant, Antico Pignolo, serves lunch and dinner and features both Venetian and international dishes.

INEXPENSIVE

Alloggi ai do Mori. Calle Larga San Marco, San Marco 658, 30124 Venezia. ☎ **041/520-4817.** Fax 041/520-5328. 11 units, 7 with bathroom. TV TEL. 130,000L ($75) double without bath, 160,000L ($93) double with bathroom. MC, V. Vaporetto: San Marco.

Don't expect an obscure corner of Venice if you check into this small-scale hotel—it's about 10 paces from Europe's densest concentration of tourists. You'll have to balance your need for space with your love of panoramas (and your ability to climb stairs, since there's no elevator), as the lower-level rooms of this 1450 town house are larger but don't have any decent views, while the rooms on the third and fourth floors are cramped but have sweeping panoramas over the basilica's domes. The site is frequently upgraded, rewallpapered, and repainted by owner Antonella Bernardi. The furniture in the rooms is simple and modern, and most of the street noise is muffled thanks to double-paned windows. The dozens of cafes in the neighborhood make up for the fact that no meals are served.

Boston Hotel. Ponte dei Dai, San Marco 848, 30124 Venezia. ☎ **041/5-28-76-65.** Fax 041/5-22-66-28. 42 units. TEL. 200,000L–290,000L ($116–$168.20) double. Rates include buffet breakfast. AE, DC, MC, V. Closed Nov–Feb. Vaporetto: San Marco.

Built in 1962, the Boston is just a whisper away from St. Mark's. The hotel was named after an uncle who left to seek his fortune in Boston and never returned. The little living rooms combine the old and the new, containing many antiques and Venetian ceilings. For the skinny guest, there's a tiny self-operated elevator and a postage stamp–sized street entrance. Most of the rooms, with parquet floors, have built-in features, snugly designed beds, chests, and wardrobes. Several even have tiny balconies that open onto canals. Twenty rooms are air-conditioned and twenty are equipped with TVs.

Hotel Riva. Ponte dell'Angelo, San Marco 5310, 30122 Venezia. ☎ **041/5-22-70-34.** 19 units, 16 with bath. 120,000L ($69.60) double without bath, 150,000L ($87) double with bath; 215,000L ($124.70) triple with bath. Rates include breakfast. No credit cards. Vaporetto: San Marco.

This small hotel is in a quiet corner only marginally removed from the hub of St. Mark's Square. One of the three narrow canals that merge in front of it first passes under the Ponte dei Sospiri (Bridge of Sighs) before reaching here. A good-value choice for this high-rent neighborhood, all three floors of rooms have been gutted and re-done, with new windows and reinforced walls, most with small marble-tiled baths. The top-floor rooms have the original wood-beamed ceilings and lovely roofscape views; open your windows and listen to the gondoliers' serenades.

3 Cannaregio

EXPENSIVE

Hotel Giorgione. Campo SS. Apostoli, Cannaregio 4586, 30131 Venezia. ☎ **041/5-22-58-10.** Fax 041/5-23-90-92. www.hotelgiorgione.com. E-mail: giorgione@hotelgiorgione.com. 78 units. A/C MINIBAR TV TEL. 190,000L–380,000L ($110.20–$220.40) double; 390,000L–420,000L ($226.20–$243.60) suite. Rates include buffet breakfast. AE, DC, MC, V. Vaporetto: Ca' d'Oro.

Despite modernization, the decor here is traditionally Venetian. The lounges and public rooms are equipped with fine furnishings and decorative accessories, and the comfortable and stylish guest rooms are designed to coddle guests. The hotel also has a typical Venetian garden. It's rated second class by the government, but the Giorgione maintains higher standards than many of the first-class places.

Dining: Breakfast is the only meal served, but many trattorie lie nearby.

Amenities: 24-hour room service, concierge, dry cleaning/laundry, baby-sitting, twice-daily maid service, small pool, business center, conference rooms, secretarial services.

MODERATE

Hotel Abbazia. Calle Priulli 68, 30121 Venezia. ☎ **041/717-949.** 39 units. TV TEL. 180,000L–310,000L ($104.40–$179.80) double. Rates include breakfast. AE, DC, MC, V. Vaporetto: Ferrovia.

Only a handful of hotels lie closer to the rail station. The benefit for travelers is that there's no need to transfer onto any vaporetto, as the hotel is accessible entirely by bridge and street from the station, which lies within a 10-minute walk. This dignified structure was built in 1889 as a monastery for barefoot Carmelite monks, who established a verdant garden in the courtyard. The garden is a most appealing spot, planted with subtropical plants that seem to thrive almost miraculously, sheltered from the cold Adriatic winds by the surrounding building. There's no restaurant on the premises and no bar, though drinks can be brought to you in the lobby. You'll find a highly accommodating staff and comfortable but unfrilly rooms that retain some of their original ascetic sobriety. Most of them (25) overlook the courtyard, ensuring quiet in an otherwise noisy neighborhood.

Hotel Geremia. Campo San Geremia, Cannaregio 290A, 30121 Venezia. ☎ **041/716-245.** Fax 041/524-2342. 20 units, 14 with bath. TV TEL. 125,000L ($72.50) double without bath, 190,000L ($110.20) double with bath. Rates include breakfast. Discounts of 20% in winter. AE, MC, V. Vaporetto: Ferrovie.

For years, the small Geremia survived as a low-cost, one-star hotel many guests considered worthy of two-star status. In 1997, the government finally raised it to two stars, justifying an almost immediate increase in rates. In a modernized turn-of-the-century setting, this hotel is a 5-minute walk from the rail station. You'll find well-maintained pale-green rooms (none with water views but all with safes). There's no elevator, but no one can deny that the price is appealing.

INEXPENSIVE

✪ **Hotel Bernardi-Semenzato.** Calle de l'Oca, Cannaregio 4366, 30121 Venezia. ☎ **041/522-7257.** Fax 041/522-2424. Hotel, 18 units, 10 with bath; annex, 8 units, 1 with bath. A/C TV TEL. 75,000L ($44) double without bath, 120,000L ($70) double with bath; 105,000L ($61) triple without bath, 130,000L ($76) triple with bath. MC, V. Closed Nov 20–Dec 10. Vaporetto: Ca' d'Oro.

From the outside, this weather-worn palazzo doesn't hint of its full 1995 renovation, which left hand-hewn ceiling beams exposed, air-conditioned rooms with coordinated headboard/spread sets, and baths modernized and brightly retiled. The enthusiastic English-speaking owners, Maria Teresa and Leonardo Pepoli, aspire to three-star style and had just received a two-star rating at press time, but they offer one-star rates (which are even less off-season). The addition of an annex 3 blocks away offers the chance to feel as if you've rented an aristocratic apartment. Most of the annex's large bathless rooms should have baths added by the time you arrive. (To get the rates above, be sure to mention you're a Frommer's reader when you're booking.)

4 On or Near Riva degli Schiavoni

VERY EXPENSIVE

⭕ **Danieli Royal Excelsior.** Riva degli Schiavoni, Castello 4196, 30122 Venezia. ☎ **800/325-3535** in the U.S. and Canada, or 041/5-22-64-80. Fax 041/5-20-02-08. www.luxurycollection.com. 240 units. A/C MINIBAR TV TEL. 670,000L–850,000L ($388.60–$493) double; 950,000L–3,700,000L ($551–$2,146) suite. Rates include buffet breakfast. AE, DC, MC, V. Vaporetto: San Zaccaria.

The Danieli was built as a grand showcase by the Doge Dandolo in the 14th century and in 1822 was transformed into a deluxe "hotel for kings." It's the most ornate hotel in Venice, surpassed only by the Cipriani and Gritti Palace. Placed in a most spectacular position, right on the Grand Canal, it has sheltered not only kings but princes, cardinals, ambassadors, and such literary figures as George Sand and Charles Dickens.

You enter into a 4-story stairwell, with Venetian arches and balustrades. The atmosphere is luxurious throughout—even the balconies opening off the main lounge are illuminated by stained-glass skylights. The rooms range widely in price, dimension, decor, and vistas, and those opening onto the lagoon cost a lot more. Alfred de Musset and Ms. Sand made love in room no. 10, the most requested accommodation at the Danieli.

Dining/Diversions: From the rooftop Terrazza Danieli, you have an unblocked view of the canals and "crowns" of Venice. There's also an intimate cocktail lounge and a bar offering piano music.

Amenities: 24-hour room service, baby-sitting, laundry/valet; hotel launch to the Lido in summer.

EXPENSIVE

Hotel Bisanzio. Calle della Pietà, Castello 3651, 30122 Venezia. ☎ **800/528-1234** in the U.S., or 041/520-3100. Fax 041/520-4114. www.bisanzio.com. E-mail: email@bisanzio.com. 47 units. A/C MINIBAR TV TEL. 350,000L ($203) double. Rates include buffet breakfast. AE, DC, MC, V. Vaporetto: San Zaccaria.

A few steps from St. Mark's Square, this hotel in the former home of sculptor Alessandro Vittoria offers hospitality and good service. It has an elevator and terraces, plus a little bar and a mooring for gondolas and motorboats. The rooms are generally quiet, each decorated in a Venetian antique style. The lounge opens onto a traditional courtyard. Amenities include 24-hour room service, baby-sitting, and laundry.

Hotel Savoia & Jolanda. Riva degli Schiavoni, Castello 4187, 30122 Venezia. ☎ **041/520-6644.** Fax 041/520-7494. 83 units. TEL. 300,000L–350,000L

($174–$203) double; from 450,000L ($261) suite. Rates include breakfast. AE, DC, MC, V. Vaporetto: San Zaccaria.

The Savoia & Jolanda occupies a prize position on Venice's main street, with a lagoon at its front yard. It opened at the turn of the century as one of the most prominent hotels along Riva degli Schiavoni, transformed from a palazzo. Though its exterior reflects much of old Venice, the interior is somewhat spiritless; the staff, however, makes life comfortable. Most of the modern rooms have a view of the boats and the Lido; they contain desks and armchairs. An addition holds 20 units with air-conditioning, phones, minibars, and TVs.

Dining: The hotel restaurant, Principessa, is open daily for lunch and dinner, serving specialties like spaghetti Bragozo with mussels and clams.

Amenities: 24-hour room service, concierge, laundry/dry cleaning, conference center.

✪ **Londra Palace.** Riva degli Schiavoni, Castello 4171, 30122 Venezia. ☎ **041/5-20-05-33.** Fax 041/5-22-50-32. www.italyhotel.com/venezia.londrapalace. 70 units. A/C MINIBAR TV TEL. 320,000L–620,000L ($185.60–$359.60) double; 520,000L–780,000L ($301.60–$452.40) junior suite. Rates include breakfast. AE, DC, MC, V. Vaporetto: San Zaccaria.

The Londra is a gabled manor with 100 windows on the lagoon, a few yards from Piazza San Marco. The hotel's most famous patron was Tchaikovsky, who wrote his Fourth Symphony in room no. 108 in December 1877; he also composed several other works here. The cozy reading room off the main lobby is reminiscent of an English club, boasting leaded windows and paneled walls with framed blow-ups of some of Tchaikovsky's sheet music. The guest rooms are luxurious, often with lacquered Venetian furniture. Romantics ask for one of the two attic rooms decorated in the Regency style with beamed ceilings. The courtyard rooms are quieter and cheaper, opening onto rooftop views instead of the Grand Canal.

Dining/Diversions: The hotel has a popular piano bar and an excellent restaurant, Do Leoni.

Amenities: 24-hour room service, baby-sitting, laundry/valet, conference hall.

MODERATE

Hotel Campiello. Campiello del Vin, Castello 4647, 30122 Venezia. ☎ **041/5-20-57-64.** Fax 041/5-20-57-98. www.hcampiello.com. 16 units. A/C TV TEL. 200,000L–250,000L ($116–$145) double. Rates include continental breakfast. Rates about 30% lower off-season. AE, MC, V. Closed Jan 7–27. Vaporetto: San Zaccaria.

This pink-fronted Venetian town house dates from the 1400s, but today you'll find cost-conscious Venetian-style accommodations last renovated in the mid-1990s. Though rated only two stars by the tourist office, it's better than its status implies, because of a spectacular location nearly adjacent to the more expensive hotels and because of Renaissance touches like marble mosaic floors and polished hardwoods. Elderly or infirm guests sometimes opt for the only room with a separate entrance, a ground-floor hideaway that fortunately has been flooded by high tides only once during the previous century. Breakfast is the only meal served.

INEXPENSIVE

Doni Pensione. Calle de Vin, Castello 4656, 30122 Venezia. ☎ **041/5-22-42-67.** Fax 041/5-22-42-67. 15 units, 3 with bath. 110,000L ($63.80) double without bath. 150,000L ($87) double with bath. Rates include breakfast. No credit cards. Vaporetto: San Zaccaria.

The Doni sits in a tranquil position, about a 3-minute walk from St. Mark's. Most of its very basic rooms overlook either a little canal, where four or five gondolas are usually tied up, or a garden with a tall fig tree. Simplicity and cleanliness prevail, especially in the down-to-earth guest rooms.

La Residenza. Campo Bandiera e Moro, Castello 3608, 30122 Venezia. ☎ **041/5-28-53-15.** Fax 041/5-23-88-59. 16 units. MINIBAR TV TEL. 150,000L–230,000L ($87–$133.40) double. Rates include breakfast. AE, DC, MC, V. Vaporetto: Arsenale.

La Residenza is in a 14th-century building that looks a lot like a miniature Doge's Palace. It's on a residential square where children play soccer and older people feed the pigeons. After gaining access (press the button outside the entrance), you'll pass through a stone vestibule lined with ancient Roman columns before ringing another bell at the bottom of a flight of stairs. First an iron gate and then a door will open into an enormous salon filled with elegant antiques, 300-year-old paintings, and some of the most marvelously preserved walls in Venice. The guest rooms are far less opulent than the public salons, with contemporary pieces and functional accessories. The choice ones are usually booked far in advance, especially for Carnevale.

5 Castello

INEXPENSIVE

Hotel Piave. Ruga Giuffa, Castello 4838–40, 30122 Venezia. ☎ **041/5-28-51-74.** Fax 041/5-23-85-12. www.elmoro.com/alpiave. 15 units. A/C. 170,000L–220,000L ($98.60–$127.60) double; 300,000L–400,000L

($174–$232) quad or 2-bedroom apt. Rates include continental breakfast. AE, DC, MC, V. Vaporetto: San Zaccaria.

The Puppin family's tasteful small hotel is a steal at these prices: This level of graciousness coupled with *buon gusto* in decor and ambience is a rare find in Venice's one-star category. A discerning, savvy crowd seems to have ferreted out this pretty spot, so you'll need to reserve far in advance. It's on a busy store-lined street a 10-minute walk northeast of Piazza San Marco, so you may have a hard time finding it the first time, but it's well worth the search. Pack light and just ask any local to point you in the direction of the Ruga Giuffa.

6   San Polo

EXPENSIVE

Hotel Rialto. Riva del Ferro, San Polo 5149, 30124 Venezia. ☎ **041/5-20-91-66.** Fax 041/5-23-89-58. www.nettuno.it/fiera/hotelrialto. E-mail: hotelrialto@nettuno.it. 77 units. A/C MINIBAR TV TEL. 250,000L–400,000L ($145–$232) double. Rates include breakfast. AE, DC, MC, V. Vaporetto: Rialto.

The Rialto opens right onto the Grand Canal at the foot of the Ponte di Rialto, the famous bridge flanked with shops. Its rooms are quite satisfactory, combining modern or Venetian furniture with ornate Venetian ceilings and wall decorations. The hotel has been considerably upgraded to second class, and private baths have been installed. The most desirable and expensive double rooms overlook the Grand Canal—these go first.

Dining/Diversions: The dining room and its adjacent bar are open daily April to October.

Amenities: Room service (7am to midnight), concierge, newspaper delivery on request.

MODERATE

Hotel Carpaccio. San Tomà, San Polo 2765, 30125 Venezia. ☎ **041/5-23-59-46.** Fax 041/5-24-21-34. 20 units. MINIBAR TV TEL. 310,000L ($179.80) double. Rates include breakfast. MC, V. Closed mid-Nov to Feb. Vaporetto: San Tomà.

Don't be put off by the narrow winding alleys that lead to the wrought-iron entrance of this second-class hotel—the building was meant to be approached by gondola. Once inside, you'll realize that your location in the heart of the oldest part of the city justifies the confusing arrival. This used to be the Palazzo Barbarigo della Terrazza, and part of it is still reserved for private apartments. The tasteful and spacious guest rooms are filled with serviceable furniture. The salon is decorated with gracious pieces, marble floors, and an arched window overlooking the Grand Canal. Breakfast is the only meal served.

Hotel Marconi. Riva del Vin, San Polo 729, 30125 Venezia. ☎ **041/5-22-20-68.** Fax 041/5-22-97-00. www.italyhotel.com/hotelm/705.html. 26 units. A/C MINIBAR TV TEL. 173,000L–344,000L ($100.35–$199.50) double. Rates include breakfast. AE, MC, V. Vaporetto: Rialto.

The Marconi, less than 50 feet from the Rialto Bridge, was built in 1500 when Venice was at the height of its supremacy. The drawing-room furnishings would be appropriate for visiting archbishops, and the Maschietto family operates everything efficiently. Only four of the lovely old rooms open onto the Grand Canal, and these, of course, are the most eagerly sought. Meals are usually taken in an L-shaped room with Gothic chairs, but in fair weather the sidewalk tables facing the Grand Canal are preferred by many.

✪ **Locanda Sturion.** Calle del Sturion, San Polo 679, 30125 Venezia. ☎ **041/523-6243.** Fax 041/522-8378. E-mail: sturion@tin.it. 11 units. A/C MINIBAR TV TEL. 200,000L–310,000L ($116–$179.80) double. Rates include continental breakfast. AE, DC, MC, V. Vaporetto: Rialto.

In the early 1200s, the Venetian doges commissioned a site where foreign merchants, who traded goods at the time near the Rialto Bridge, could stay for the night after a hard day's bargaining. After long stints as a private residence, the site continues its tradition of catering to foreign visitors. A private entrance leads up four steep flights of marble steps, past apartments on the lower floors, to a labyrinth of cozy, clean, but not overly large guest rooms. Most have views over the terra-cotta rooftops of this congested neighborhood; two, however, open onto views of the Grand Canal. The intimate breakfast room is a honey—almost like a parlor with red brocaded walls, a Venetian chandelier, and a trio of big windows opening onto the Grand Canal.

7 Santa Croce

MODERATE

✪ **Hotel San Cassiano Ca' Favretto.** Calle della Regina, Santa Croce 2232, 30135 Venezia. ☎ **041/5-24-17-68.** Fax 041/72-10-33. www.italyhotel.com/hotelm/711.html. E-mail: cassiano@cassiano.it. 36 units. A/C MINIBAR TV TEL. 200,000L–344,000L ($116–$199.50) double. Rates include breakfast. AE, DC, MC, V. Vaporetto: San Stae.

This hotel used to be the studio of 19th-century painter Giacomo Favretto. The gondola pier and the dining room porch both afford views of the lacy facade of the Ca' d'Oro, perhaps the most beautiful building in Venice. The building is a former 14th-century palace, and the present owner has worked closely with Venetian authorities to preserve the original details, like a 20-foot beamed ceiling in the entrance area. Fifteen of the conservatively decorated rooms overlook one of two canals, and many are filled with antiques or high-quality reproductions.

8 Dorsoduro

MODERATE

American Hotel. Campo San Vio, Dorsoduro 628, 30123 Venezia. ☎ **041/5-20-47-33.** Fax 041/5-20-40-48. E-mail: hotelameri@tin.it. 29 units. A/C MINIBAR TV TEL. 340,000L ($197.20) double; 400,000L ($232) triple. Rates include breakfast. AE, DC, MC, V. Vaporetto: Accademia.

On a small waterway, the American (there's nothing American about it) lies in an ocher building across the Grand Canal from the most heavily touristed areas. It's one of your best budget bets in Venice. The modest lobby is filled with murals, warm colors, and antiques, and the location is perfect for anyone wanting to avoid the crowds that descend on Venice in summer. The rooms are comfortably furnished in a Venetian style, but they vary in size; some of the smaller ones are a bit cramped. Many rooms with their own private terrace face the canal. On the second floor is a beautiful terrace where guests can relax over drinks. The staff is attentive and helpful.

Hotel La Calcina. Fondamenta Zàttere ai Gesuati, Dorsoduro 780, 30123 Venezia. ☎ **041/5-20-64-66.** Fax 041/5-22-70-45. 29 units. A/C TEL. 170,000L–280,000L ($98.60–$162.40) double. Rates include buffet breakfast. AE, MC, V. Vaporetto: Zàttere.

Recently renovated (and just in time!), La Calcina lies in a secluded and less-trampled district that used to be the English enclave before the area developed a broader base of tourism. John Ruskin, who wrote *The Stones of Venice,* stayed here in 1877, and he charted the ground for his latter-day compatriots. This pensione is absolutely spotless, and the furnishings are well chosen but hardly elaborate. The rooms are cozy and comfortable.

✪ **Pensione Accademia.** Fondamenta Bollani, Dorsoduro 1058, 30123 Venezia. ☎ **041/5-23-78-46.** Fax 041/5-23-91-52. 27 units. 190,000L–330,000L ($110.20–$191.40) double. Rates include breakfast. AE, DC, MC, V. Vaporetto: Accademia.

The Accademia is the most patrician of the pensioni, in a villa whose garden extends into an angle created by the junction of two canals. The interior features Gothic-style paneling, Venetian chandeliers, and Victorian-era furniture. The building served as the Russian

Embassy before World War II and as a private house before that. There's an upstairs sitting room flanked by two large windows and a formal rose garden. The spacious guest rooms are decorated with original furniture from the 19th century. Some are air-conditioned and most have been renovated. This was the fictional residence of Katharine Hepburn's character in the film *Summertime*.

INEXPENSIVE

✪ **Locanda Montini.** Fondamenta di Borgo, Dorsoduro 1147, 31000 Venezia. ☎ **041/5-22-71-51.** Fax 041/5-20-02-55. 10 units, 3 with bath. 90,000L ($52.20) double without bath, 100,000L ($58) double with bath. AE, DC, MC, V. Vaporetto: Accademia.

The Montin is an old-fashioned Venetian inn whose adjoining restaurant is one of the most loved in the area. It's officially listed as a fourth-class hotel, but the rooms are considerably larger and better than that rating would suggest. Reservations are virtually mandatory because of its reputation. The inn is a bit difficult to locate—it's marked by only a small carriage lamp etched with the name—but is worth the search.

9 Isola della Giudecca

VERY EXPENSIVE

✪ **Hotel Cipriani.** Isola della Giudecca 10, 30133 Venezia. ☎ **800/992-5055** in the U.S. and Canada, or 041/5-20-77-44. Fax 041/5-20-77-45. 104 units. A/C MINIBAR TV TEL. 950,000L–1,400,000L ($551–$812) double; from 2,100,000L ($1,218) suite. Rates include breakfast. AE, DC, MC, V. Closed Nov–Mar. Vaporetto: Zitelle.

With its isolated location, haute service, and exorbitant prices, the Cipriani outclasses every other posh contender, including the Danieli and Gritti Palace. Set in a 16th-century cloister on the residential island of Giudecca, this pleasure palace was opened in 1958 by Giuseppe Cipriani, the founder of Harry's Bar and the one real-life character in Hemingway's Venetian novel. The guest rooms have different amenities, ranging from tasteful contemporary to an antique design—but all have splendid views. The Cipriani, incidentally, is the only hotel on Giudecca, which otherwise is calm and quiet.

Dining: Lunch is served in the bar, Il Gabbiano, either indoors or on terraces overlooking the water. More formal meals are served at night in the restaurant.

Amenities: The best in Venice, with two employees for every room. A private launch service ferries guests, at any hour, to and from the hotel's own pier near Piazza San Marco. 24-hour room service, baby-sitting, laundry/valet; Olympic-size pool with filtered salt water, tennis courts, sauna, fitness center.

10 The Lido

VERY EXPENSIVE

✪ **Excelsior Palace.** Lungomare Marconi 41, 30126 Lido di Venezia. ☎ **800/325-3535** in the U.S. and Canada, or 041/5-26-02-01. Fax 041/5-26-72-76. www.luxurycollection.com. 214 units. A/C MINIBAR TV TEL. 605,000L–737,000L ($350.90–$427.45) double; from 1,265,000L ($733.70) suite. AE, DC, MC, V. Parking 35,000L ($20.30). Closed Nov–Mar 15. Vaporetto: Lido; then bus A, B, or C.

When the mammoth Excelsior was built, it was the biggest resort hotel of its kind in the world and did much to make the Lido fashionable. Today it offers the most luxury along the Lido, though it doesn't have the antique character of the Hotel des Bains. Its rooms range in style and amenities from cozy singles to suites. Most of the social life takes place around the angular pool or on the flowered terraces leading up to the cabanas on the sandy beach. All guest rooms (some big enough for tennis games) have been modernized, often with vivid summerlike colors.

Dining/Diversions: The hotel features one of the most elegant dining rooms of the Adriatic, the Tropicana. The Blue Bar has piano music and views of the beach.

Amenities: 24-hour room service, baby-sitting, laundry, valet; six tennis courts, pool, private pier with boat rental are available. A private launch makes hourly runs to the Gritti Palace and the Danieli on the Grand Canal.

EXPENSIVE

✪ **Hotel des Bains.** Lungomare Marconi 17, 30126 Lido di Venezia. ☎ **800/325-3535** in the U.S. and Canada, or 041/5-26-59-21. Fax 041/5-26-01-13. www.luxurycollection.com. 210 units. A/C MINIBAR TV TEL. 445,000L–700,000L ($258.10–$406) double; 700,000L–1,400,000L ($406–$812) suite. AE, DC, MC, V. Free parking. Closed Nov–Mar. Vaporetto: Lido; then bus A, B, or C.

This hotel was built in the grand era of European resort hotels, but its supremacy on the Lido was long ago lost to the Excelsior. It has its own wooded park and beach with individual cabanas. Its confectionery-like facade dates from the turn of the century. Thomas Mann stayed here several times before making it the setting for his *Death in Venice,* and later it was used as a set for the film of the same name. The renovated interior exudes the flavor of the leisurely life of the belle epoque. The guest rooms are well furnished and fairly large.

Dining: Guests can dine in a large veranda room cooled by Adriatic sea breezes. The food is top rate and the service superior.

Amenities: 24-hour room service, baby-sitting, laundry/valet. A motorboat shuttles back and forth between Venice and the Lido. Hotel guests have privileges at the Golf Club Alberoni, where many resort-type services are available (tennis courts, large pool, private pier).

✪ **Hotel Quattro Fontane.** Via Quattro Fontane 16, 30126 Lido di Venezia. ☎ **041/5-26-02-27.** Fax 041/5-26-07-26. 57 units. A/C TV TEL. 360,000L–500,000L ($208.80–$290) double. Rates include breakfast. AE, DC, MC, V. Free parking. Closed Nov–Apr 4. Vaporetto: Lido; then bus A, B, or C.

In its price bracket, the Quattro Fontane is one of the most charming hotels on the Lido. The trouble is, a lot of people know that, so it's likely to be booked. This former summer home of a 19th-century Venetian family is most popular with the British, who seem to appreciate the homelike atmosphere, the garden, the helpful staff, and the rooms with superior amenities, not to mention the good food served at tables set under shade trees. Many of the rooms are furnished with antiques.

Dining/Diversions: The dining room is open April to October. There's a bar adjacent to the restaurant.

Amenities: 24-hour room service, concierge, laundry/dry cleaning, newspaper delivery on request, twice-daily maid service. The hotel maintains changing booths and about a dozen private cabanas on the beach, a short walk away. There's also a tennis court.

MODERATE

✪ **Hotel Belvedere.** Piazzale Santa Maria Elisabetta 4, 30126 Lido di Venezia. ☎ **041/5-26-57-73.** Fax 041/5-26-14-86. 30 units. A/C TV TEL. 180,000L–295,000L ($104.40–$171.10) double. Rates include breakfast. AE, DC, MC, V. Free parking. Vaporetto: Lido.

The restored and modernized Belvedere has been run by the same family since 1857, and its restaurant is justifiably popular (see chapter 5). Right across from the vaporetto stop, the hotel is open all year, which is unusual for the Lido, and offers simply furnished rooms. All have a view of the lagoon. There's parking in its garden. As an added courtesy, the Belvedere offers guests free entrance to the Casino Municipale, and in summer guests can use the hotel's bathing huts on the Venetian Lido.

Hotel Helvetia. Gran Viale 4–6, 30126 Lido di Venezia. ☎ **041/5-26-01-05.**
Fax 041/5-26-89-03. 56 units. TEL. 180,000L–310,000L ($104.40–$179.80)
double. Rates include breakfast. MC, V. Closed Nov–Mar. Vaporetto: Lido; then
bus A, B, or C.

The Helvetia is a russet-colored 19th-century building with stone
detailing on a side street near the lagoon side of the island, an easy
walk from the vaporetto stop. The quieter rooms face away from the
street, and rooms in the older wing have belle epoque high ceilings
and attractively comfortable furniture. The newer wing is more
streamlined and has been renovated in a more conservative style.
Breakfast is served, weather permitting, in a flagstone-covered wall
garden behind the hotel. Baby-sitting, laundry, and 24-hour room
service are available.

5

Dining

*V*enice is bounded by a rich agricultural district and plentiful vine-yards. The many specialties prepared in the Venetian kitchen will be surveyed in the restaurant recommendations that follow.

Venice's restaurants are high priced compared to the rest of Italy. The city gets the choicest items on its menus from the Adriatic—but beware, the fish dishes are very expensive. Note that the price you'll see on the menu for fresh grilled fish (*pesce alla griglia*) refers to the *etto* (per 100 grams) and so is a fraction of the real cost. Have the waiter estimate the cost before you order.

Many trattorie cater to moderate budgets. Some restaurants still offer a *menu turistico* (tourist menu) at a set price. It includes soup (nearly always minestrone) or pasta, followed by a meat dish with vegetables, topped off by dessert (fresh fruit or cheese), plus a quarter liter of wine or mineral water, bread, cover charge, and service (you'll still be expected to tip). Some restaurants serve a fixed-price meal called a *menu a presso fisso,* which rarely includes the cost of your wine but does include taxes and service.

If you want only a plate of spaghetti or something light, you can patronize any number of fast-food cafeterias, *rôsticcerias,* or *tavola caldas.* You don't pay a cover charge and can order as much or as little as you wish. Pizzerias are another good option for light meals or snacks. Many bars or cafe-bars also offer both hot and cold food throughout the day. If you're lunching light in the heat, ask for *panini,* rolls stuffed with meat. *Tramezzini* are white-bread sand-wiches with the crust trimmed.

1 Best Bets

- **Best Spot for a Romantic Dinner:** If you aren't already in love, you'll fall head over heels with your dining companion at the **Locanda Cipriani,** Piazza San Fosca 29 (☎ **041/73-01-50**), on sleepy Torcello, the island in the lagoon that time forgot (see chapter 10). Opened in 1946 by Arrigo Cipriani of Harry's Bar fame, it naturally attracted Hemingway, but since then celebrities and the discriminating from all over the world have made their way here.

A Dining Note

Phone numbers of restaurants often aren't valid for more than a year or two. For reasons known only to the restaurateurs themselves, opening hours and even days of closing are changed frequently. So always check with the restaurant before heading there. If the staff doesn't speak English and you need a confirmed reservation (always a good idea), ask someone at your hotel reception desk to make a reservation for you.

- **Best Spot for a Celebration:** There's no other place in Venice that's quite as much fun as **Harry's Bar,** Calle Vallaresso, San Marco 1323 (☎ **041/5-28-57-77**). After a few of the bartender's Bellinis (white peach juice and Prosecco), you'll be in the mood to celebrate regardless of the occasion. The best time to arrive if you crave activity, laughter, crowds, and merriment is 7 to 9pm. It's the most active downstairs. And the food is great.
- **Best View:** The **Ristorante alle Zattere,** Fondamente Zaterre ai Gesuati 795 (☎ **041/520-4224**), attracts diners for its views overlooking the Canal della Giudecca. The best views are at night, when the lights and sounds make the passing throngs seem more like a Hollywood movie than reality. The cuisine isn't a bad reason for visiting either.
- **Best Wine List:** It's not only the city's most elegant restaurant and enduring favorite, but the **Antico Martini,** Campo San Fantin, San Marco 1983 (☎ **041/5-22-41-21**), has a wine list of which even Bacchus would approve.
- **Best Value:** If you're a diner of average means with better-than-average tastes, head for the **Trattoria alla Madonna,** Calle de la Madonna, San Polo 594 (☎ **041/5-22-38-24**), named for an even more famous Madonna than the singer. Since 1954 it's been feeding in-the-know locals in the Rialto area with its savory reasonably priced cuisine. Everyone flocks here, from upper-crust Venetians to singing gondoliers.
- **Best for the Kids:** Though it's in the heart of the overpriced San Marco area, **Le Chat Qui Rit,** Calle Frezzeria, San Marco 1131 (☎ **041/5-22-90-86**), still keeps decent prices and even serves good food. The cuisine isn't refined and certainly not haute, but it pleases most families. This is both a self-service cafeteria and a pizzeria, one of the few dining spots in Venice that's truly kid- and family-friendly.

- **Best Venetian Cuisine:** Deep in the heart of Venice, the aristocratic **Antico Martini,** Campo San Fantin, San Marco 1983 (☎ 041/5-22-41-21), offers up the rich bounty of the Veneto, along with the freshest fish, poultry, and meat dishes—a true journey into the robust flavors of the Venetian diet. Though culinary snobs, especially from other parts of Italy, put down the Venetian cuisine, a romantic dinner here might have you singing its praise. Begin with the "fruits of the sea," a medley of shellfish, then follow with tender veal liver fried with onions and served with yellow polenta.

- **Best International Cuisine:** The chefs at **Do Forni,** Calle dei Specchieri, San Marco 468 (☎ 041/5-23-21-48), roam the world for culinary inspiration. Though it has its detractors, Do Forni succeeds far more than it misses the mark. After all, chefs can't be experts in all cooking schools, but here they try. They're experts at Venetian cookery, however, but will also take on Moroccan, German, English, or even good old American cuisine.

- **Best Seafood:** About every sea creature from the Adriatic turns up on your platter at the **Ristorante à la Vecia Cavana,** Rio dei Terrà SS. Apostoli, Cannaregio 4624 (☎ 041/5-28-71-06), well off the tourist-trodden path. Its *zuppa di pesce* (fish soup) is among the city's best, and the fish-laden array of antipasti is worth the search to find this place. For some reason, the more hideous looking the fish, the better it seems to taste.

- **Best Pizza:** New York's claim to the best pizza is challenged by this place. When Venetians crave pizza, they head for **Pizzeria alle Oche,** Calle del Tintor, San Polo 1552B (☎ 041/524-1161), where a selection of 85 pizzas awaits them, ranging from a *quattro formaggio* (four cheese) pizza to a pear pizza. Steaks, veal, chicken, and fish are also specialties.

- **Best Desserts:** With a name like **Harry's Dolci,** Fondamenta San Biago 773, Isola della Giudecca (☎ 041/5-20-83-37), you expect the desserts to be good—and they are. Even superb. Created by the same people of Harry's Bar fame, Harry's Dolci serves the best zabaglione cake in Venice. It's worth the boat ride across the canal.

- **Best Late-Night Dining:** A lot of late-night dining around the world isn't worth the bother, with a bored, unshaven chef tossing something frozen in a vat of hot grease. But **Alfredo, Alfredo,** Campo San Felipe e Giacomi, Castello 4294 (☎ 041/5-22-53-31), feeds you adequately until 2am. It's conveniently close to

Piazza San Marco. Even after midnight, the chefs can turn out a savory spaghetti dish or various omelets and grilled meats.

- **Best Outdoor Dining:** When the lights of Venice go on, they're best viewed in all their twinkling glitter from the elegant dining terraces of the **Ristorante Cipriani,** in the Hotel Cipriani, Isola della Giudecca 10 (☎ 041/5-20-77-44), across the Grand Canal. Sitting on the terrace, sipping the last Bellini of October or tasting the first white truffle of spring, you'll think you've arrived prematurely at Heaven's Gate.

- **Best People Watching:** If you'd been sitting at the **Taverna la Fenice,** Campiello de la Fenice, San Marco 1938 (☎ 041/5-22-38-56), since it opened in 1907, you'd have seen half the cultural world of Europe parade by for your inspection. They were heading for the now burned out Teatro La Fenice. This tavern is still one of the most romantic dining spots in Venice, and the parade of humanity passing by today is at least as interesting as the divine risotto the chef prepares with scampi and arugula.

- **Best for Afternoon Tea:** If the fickle George Sand and her young lover, Alfred de Musset, were to return to Venice today, we're sure you'd find them having afternoon tea at the **Caffè Florian,** Piazza San Marco 56–59 (☎ 041/5-28-53-38). Since 1720, this has been the most famous and romantic cafe in Europe, serving everyone from Casanova to Goethe. You get not only tea along with those delectable Italian pastries and moist cakes but also all the glory of Piazza San Marco—and even live music.

- **Best Brunch:** After feeding the overstuffed pigeons on St. Mark's Square and ducking into the basilica, there remains the final delight of a late brunch at **Do Leoni,** in the Londra Palace Hotel, Riva degli Schiavoni, Castello 4171 (☎ 041/5-20-05-33). In a rich setting of scarlet and gold, you can feast on a buffet spread of hot and cold dishes, both Italian and international. After sampling your fill, sit back and linger over the lush Black Forest cake while taking in the view of the canal.

- **Best Fast Food:** Long a haven for budget travelers, the **Rosticceria San Bartolomeo,** Calle della Bissa, San Marco 5424 (☎ 041/5-22-35-69), is Venice's most frequented fast-food eatery. And with good reason. The price is right and the food good, wholesome, and plentiful. Feast on deep-fried mozzarella, polenta, or the local codfish.

- **Best Picnic Fare:** Venice makes picnic shopping easy. It's filled with shops specializing in a separate type of foodstuff: yogurt and cheese, for example, coming from a *latteria;* slices of cold ham and salami from a *salumeria;* wine from a *vinaterria;* bread from a *panneteria;* pastries from a *pasticerria;* and fresh fruits and vegetables from an *alimentaria.* These shops found all over the city are supplemented by open-air produce markets, the biggest of which is at **Campo Santa Margherita.**

2 San Marco

VERY EXPENSIVE

✪ **Harry's Bar.** Calle Vallaresso, San Marco 1323. ☎ **041/5-28-57-77.** Reservations required. Main courses 80,000L–95,000L ($46.40–$55.10). AE, DC, MC, V. Daily 10:30am–11pm. Vaporetto: San Marco. VENETIAN.

Harry's Bar serves the best food in Venice. A. E. Hotchner, in his *Papa Hemingway,* quoted the writer as saying, "We can't eat straight hamburger in a Renaissance palazzo on the Grand Canal." So he ordered a 5-pound "tin of beluga caviar" to "take the curse off it." Hemingway would probably skip the place today, and the prices would come as a shock even to him. Harry, by the way, is an Italian named Arrigo, son of the late Commendatore Cipriani. Like his father, Arrigo is an entrepreneur extraordinaire known for the standard of his cuisine. His bar is a big draw for martini-thirsty Americans, but Hemingway and Hotchner always ordered a Bloody Mary. The most famous drink is the Bellini (Prosecco and white peach juice). (Off-season, the Bellinis can become watered-down horrors—a gamble at 17,500L/$10.) You can have your choice of dining in the bar downstairs or the room with a view upstairs. We recommend the Venetian fish soup, followed by the scampi Thermidor with rice pilaf or the seafood ravioli. The food is relatively simple but absolutely fresh.

EXPENSIVE

✪ **Antico Martini.** Campo San Fantin, San Marco 1983. ☎ **041/5-22-41-21.** Reservations required. Main courses 36,000L–55,000L ($20.90–$31.90); fixed-price menu 40,000L–55,000L ($23.20–$31.90) at lunch, 72,000L–98,000L ($41.75–$56.85) at dinner. AE, DC, MC, V. Wed 7–11:30pm, Thurs–Mon noon–2:30pm and 7–11:30pm. Vaporetto: San Marco or Santa Maria del Giglio. VENETIAN/INTERNATIONAL.

Antico Martini, the city's leading restaurant, elevates Venetian cuisine to its highest level. Elaborate chandeliers glitter and gilt-framed oil paintings adorn the paneled walls. The courtyard is splendid in summer. An excellent beginning is the risotto di frutti di mare (fresh seafood) in a creamy Venetian style. For a main dish, try the fegato alla veneziana, tender liver fried with onions and served with polenta, a yellow cornmeal mush. The chefs are better at regional dishes than at international ones. The restaurant has one of the city's best wine lists, featuring more than 350 wines. The yellow Tocai is an interesting local wine and especially good with fish dishes.

Da Ivo. Calle dei Fuseri, San Marco 1809. ☎ **041/5-28-50-04.** Reservations required. Main courses 30,000L–100,000L ($17.40–$58). AE, DC, MC, V. Mon–Sat noon–2:30pm and 7–11pm. Closed Jan 6–31. Vaporetto: San Marco. TUSCAN/VENETIAN.

Da Ivo has such a faithful crowd you'll think at first you're in a semi-private club. The rustic atmosphere is cozy and relaxing, and your well-set table is bathed in candlelight. Florentines head here for fine Tuscan cookery, but regional Venetian dishes are also served. In season, game, prepared according to ancient traditions, is cooked over an open charcoal grill. One cold December day our hearts and plates were warmed by an order of a homemade tagliatelli topped with slivers of tartufi bianchi, the unforgettable pungent white truffle from Piedmont. Dishes change according to the season and the availability of ingredients but are likely to include swordfish, anglerfish, a stew pot of fish, or cuttlefish in its own ink.

La Caravella. In the Hotel Saturnia International, Calle Larga XXII Marzo, San Marco 2398. ☎ 041/5-20-89-01. Reservations required. Main courses 44,000L–80,000L ($25.50–$46.40); fixed-price lunch 85,000L ($49.30). AE, DC, MC, V. Daily noon–3pm and 7pm–midnight. Vaporetto: San Marco. VENETIAN/INTERNATIONAL.

La Caravella has an overblown nautical atmosphere and a leather-bound menu that may make you think you're in a tourist trap. It may be expensive, but it's not a trap: It's a citadel of good food and wine. The restaurant contains four dining rooms and a courtyard for summer. The decor is rustically elegant, with frescoed ceilings, bouquets of flowers, and wrought-iron lighting fixtures. Many of the specialties are featured nowhere else in town. You might begin with an antipasti misto de pesce (fish) with olive oil and lemon juice or prawns with avocado. Two star specialties are granceola (Adriatic sea crab on carpaccio) and chateaubriand for two. The best item to order, however, is one of the poached fish, such as bass–priced according to weight and served with a tempting sauce. The ice cream in champagne is a soothing finish.

Quadri. Piazza San Marco, San Marco 120–124. ☎ **041/5-22-21-05.** Reservations required. Main courses 45,000L–69,000L ($26.10–$40). AE, DC, MC, V. Wed–Sun noon–2:30pm and 7–10:30pm; Tues 7–10:30pm. Vaporetto: San Marco. INTERNATIONAL.

Venice Dining

Legend
Church ✝

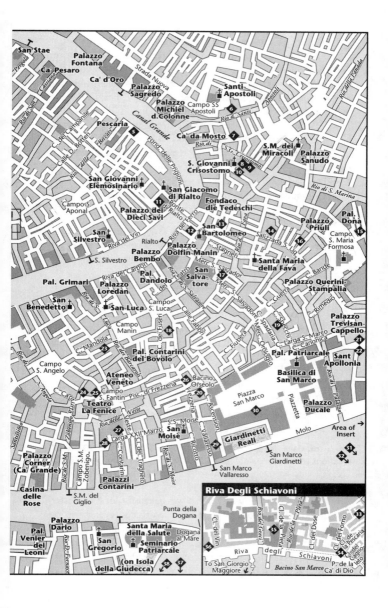

San'Stae
Palazzo Fontana
Ca' Pesaro
Ca' d'Oro
Palazzo Sagredo
Palazzo Michiel d.Colonne
Santi Apostoli
Campo SS Apostoli **6**
Pescaria **5**
Canal Grande
Strada Nuova
Ca' da Mosto **7**
Rio di
S.M. dei Miracoli
Palazzo Sanudo
S. Giovanni Crisostomo **8 9 10**
San Giovanni Elemosinario
San Giacomo di Rialto **11**
Fondaco die Tedeschi
Campo S Aponal
Palazzo dei Dieci Savi
Palazzo Priuli
Pal. Dona
San Silvestro
San Bartolomeo **12 13**
Salizzada S. Lio **14**
Campo S. Maria Formosa
15
16
S. Silvestro
Rialto
Riva del Vin
Palazzo Bembo
Palazzo Dolfin-Manin
Santa Maria della Fava
Riva del Carbon
San Salvatore **17**
Pal. Grimari
Palazzo Loredan
Pal. Dandolo
Palazzo Querini-Stampalia
San Benedetto
San Luca
Campo S. Luca
Palazzo Trevisan-Cappello **21 22**
Campo Manin
18
19
Sant Apollonia
23
Pal. Contarini del'Bovolo
Pal. Patriarcale
Campo S. Angelo
Ateneo Veneto
26
Bacino Orseolo
Basilica di San Marco
24 25
Campo S. Fantin
Teatro La Fenice
20
Piazza San Marco
Palazzo Ducale
30
Piazzetta
San Moise
27
28
Larga XXII Marzo
29
Giardinetti Reali
Molo
Area of Insert
Palazzo Corner (Ca' Grande)
Palazzi Contarini
San Marco Giardinetti
31
32
Casina delle Rose
S.M. del Giglio
Punta della Dogana
San Marco Vallaresso
Palazzo Dario
Santa Maria della Salute
Dogana al Mare
33
Pal. Venier dei Leoni
San Gregorio
Seminario Patriarcale
35
36
Riva degli Schiavoni
34
Riva Degli Schiavoni
(on Isola della Giudecca) **38 37**
To San Giorgio Maggiore
Bacino San Marco
Ca' di Dio

One of Europe's most famous restaurants, Quadri is even better known as a cafe (see chapter 9). This deluxe place, with its elegant decor and crowd, overlooks the "living room" of Venice. Many diners come just for the view and are often surprised by the memorable setting, high-quality cuisine, and impeccable service. Harry's Bar and Antico Martini have better food, though the chef's skills are considerable. It's often packed with celebrities during art and film festivals, the world glitterati taking delight in this throwback to the days of La Serenissima. The chef is likely to tempt you with such dishes as scallops with saffron, salt codfish with polenta, marinated swordfish, or sea bass with crab sauce. Dessert specialties are "baked" ice cream and lemon mousse with fresh strawberry sauce.

MODERATE

"Al Graspo de Uva." Calle dei Bombaseri, San Marco 5094. ☎ **041/5-20-01-50.** Reservations required. Main courses 26,000L–35,000L ($15.10–$20.30). AE, DC, V. Wed–Sun 12:15–3pm and 7:45–10:45pm. Closed Jan 2–17. Vaporetto: Rialto. SEAFOOD/VENETIAN.

"Al Graspo de Uva" is one bunch of grapes you'll want to pluck. Near the Rialto Bridge, it's a winner for that special meal. Decorated in the old taverna style, it offers several air-conditioned dining rooms. One has a beamed ceiling, hung with garlic and copper bric-a-brac. Among the best fish restaurants in Venice, "Al Graspo de Uva" has been patronized by Elizabeth Taylor, Jeanne Moreau, and even Giorgio de Chirico. You can help yourself to all the hors d'oeuvres you want—known on the menu as "self-service mammoth." Next try the gran fritto dell'Adriatico, a mixed treat of deep-fried fish from the Adriatic. The desserts are also good, especially the peach Melba.

✪ **Do Forni.** Calle dei Specchieri, San Marco 468. ☎ **041/5-23-21-48.** Reservations required. Main courses 25,000L–40,000L ($14.50–$23.20). AE, DC, MC, V. Daily noon–4pm and 6pm–midnight. Vaporetto: San Marco. INTERNATIONAL/VENETIAN.

Centuries ago, this was where bread was baked for local monasteries, but today it's the busiest restaurant in Venice—even when the rest of the city slumbers under a wintertime Adriatic fog. It's divided into two sections, separated by a narrow alley. The Venetian cognoscenti prefer the front part, decorated in Orient Express style. The larger section in back is like a country tavern, with ceiling beams and original paintings. The English menu (with at least 80 dishes from which to choose, prepared by a team of 14 cooks) is titled "food for the gods" and lists such specialties as spider crab in its own shell, risotto primavera, linguine with rabbit, and sea bass en papillote (parchment). The food is international in scope.

Ristorante da Raffaele. Calle Larga XXII Marzo, San Marco 2347 (Fondamenta delle Ostreghe). ☎ **041/5-23-23-17.** Reservations recommended. Main courses 20,000L–35,000L ($11.60–$20.30). AE, DC, MC, V. Fri–Wed noon–3pm and 7–11pm. Closed Dec 10 to mid-Feb. Vaporetto: San Marco or Santa Maria del Giglio. ITALIAN/VENETIAN.

The Raffaele, a 5-minute walk from Piazza San Marco, has long been a favorite canal-side restaurant. It's often overrun with tourists, but the veteran kitchen staff handles the onslaught well. Dating from 1953, the restaurant offers the kind of charm and atmosphere unique to Venice. The huge inner sanctum has a high-beamed ceiling, 17th- to 19th-century pistols and sabers, exposed brick, wrought-iron chandeliers, a massive fireplace, and copper pots (hundreds of them). The food is excellent, beginning with a choice of tasty antipasti or well-prepared pastas. Seafood specialties include scampi, squid, and deep-fried fish from the Adriatic. The grilled meats are wonderful. Finish with a tempting dessert. The crowded conviviality is part of the experience.

✪ **Taverna la Fenice.** Campiello de la Fenice, San Marco 1938. ☎ **041/5-22-38-56.** Reservations required. Main courses 18,000L–32,000L ($10.45–$18.55). AE, DC, MC, V. Aug–Apr Mon 7–10:30pm, Tues–Sat noon–2:30pm and 7–10:30pm; May–July daily noon–2:30pm and 7–10:30pm. Closed 2nd week in Jan. Vaporetto: San Marco. ITALIAN/VENETIAN.

Opened in 1907, when Venetians were flocking in record numbers to hear the bel canto performances in nearby La Fenice opera house (which burned down a few years ago), this restaurant is one of Venice's most romantic dining spots. The interior is suitably elegant, but the preferred spot in clement weather is outdoors beneath a canopy. The service is smooth and efficient. The most appetizing beginning is the selection of seafood antipasti. The fish is fresh from the Mediterranean. You might enjoy the risotto con scampi e arugula, tagliatelle with cream sauce and exotic mushrooms, John Dory filets with butter and lemon, turbot roasted with potatoes and tomato sauce, scampi with tomatoes and rice, or carpaccio alla Fenice.

Trattoria la Colomba. Piscina Frezzeria, San Marco 1665. ☎ **041/5-22-11-75.** Reservations recommended. Main courses 40,000L–75,000L ($23.20–$43.50). AE, DC, MC, V. Daily noon–2:30pm and 7–11:30pm. Closed Wed June 19–Aug and Nov–Apr. Vaporetto: San Marco or Rialto. VENETIAN/INTERNATIONAL.

This is one of the most distinctive trattorie in town, with a history that's more than 100 years old and a legendary association with some of Venice's leading painters. In 1985, a $2 million restoration improved the place, making it a more attractive foil for the modern paintings adorning its walls (they change seasonally and are for sale). Menu items are likely to include at least five daily specials based on Venice's time-honored cuisine as well as risotto di funghi del Montello (risotto with mushrooms from the local hills of Montello) and baccalà alla vicentina (milk-simmered dry cod seasoned with onions, anchovies, and cinnamon and served with polenta). The fruits and vegetables used in the dishes are for the most part grown on the lagoon islands.

Vini da Arturo. Calle degli Assassini, San Marco 3656. ☎ **041/5-28-69-74.** Reservations recommended. Main courses 28,000L–43,000L ($16.25–$24.95). No credit cards. Mon–Sat noon–2:30pm and 7–10:30pm. Closed Aug. Vaporetto: San Marco or Rialto. VENETIAN.

Vini da Arturo attracts many devoted regulars to its seven tables, including artists and writers. You get delectable local cooking—not just the standard clichés and not seafood, which may be unique for a Venetian restaurant. One restaurant owner, who likes to dine here occasionally instead of at his own place, explained, "The subtle difference between good and bad food is often nothing more than the amount of butter and cream used." Instead of ordering plain pasta, try the tantalizing spaghetti alla Gorgonzola. The beef is also good, especially when prepared with a cream sauce flavored with mustard and pepper. The salads are made with fresh ingredients, often in unusual combinations; particularly interesting is the pappardelle radicchio.

INEXPENSIVE

⭘ **Le Chat Qui Rit.** Calle Frezzeria, San Marco 1131. ☎ **041/5-22-90-86.** Main courses 10,000L–16,000L ($5.80–$9.30); pizza 9,000L–14,000L ($5.20–$8.10). No credit cards. Nov–Aug Sun–Fri 11am–9:30pm; Sept–Oct daily 11am–9:30pm. Vaporetto: San Marco. VENETIAN/PIZZA.

This self-service cafeteria/pizzeria offers food prepared "just like Mama made." It's very popular because of its low prices. Dishes might include cuttlefish simmered in stock and served on a bed of yellow polenta or various fried fish. You can also order a steak grilled very simply, flavored with oil, salt, and pepper or a little garlic and herbs if you prefer. Main-dish platters are served rather quickly after you order them.

⭘ **Rosticceria San Bartolomeo.** Calle della Bissa, San Marco 5424. ☎ **041/5-22-35-69.** Main courses 12,000L–25,000L ($6.95–$14.50); fixed-price menu 32,000L–42,000L ($18.55–$24.35). AE, MC, V. Tues–Sun 10am–2:30pm and 5–9pm. Vaporetto: Rialto. VENETIAN.

This rôsticceria is Venice's most frequented fast-food place and has long been a haven for cost-conscious travelers. Downstairs is a tavola calda where you can eat standing up, but upstairs is a restaurant with waiter service. Typical dishes are baccalà alla vicentina (codfish simmered in herbs and milk), deep-fried mozzarella (which the Italians call carrozza), and seppie con polenta (squid in its own ink sauce, served with polenta). Everything is accompanied with typical Veneto wine.

Once you leave the vaporetto, take an underpass on your left (with your back facing the bridge). This passageway is labeled SOTTOPORTEGO DELLA BISSA. The restaurant will be at the first corner, off Campo San Bartolomeo.

Sempione. Ponte Beretteri, San Marco 578. ☎ **041/522-6022.** Reservations recommended. Main courses 17,600L–31,000L ($10.20–$18). AE, DC, MC, V. Daily 11:30am–3pm and 6:30–10pm. Closed Jan. Vaporetto: Rialto. VENETIAN.

This restaurant has done an admirable job of feeding locals and visitors for almost 90 years. Set adjacent to a canal in a 15th-century building near Piazza San Marco, it contains three dining rooms done in a soothingly traditional style, a well-trained staff, and a kitchen focusing on traditional Venetian cuisine. Examples are grilled fish, spaghetti with crabmeat, risotto with fish, fish soup, and a delectable version of Venetian calve's liver that hasn't been significantly changed since the restaurant was founded. Try for a table by the window so you can watch the gondolas glide by.

3 Cannaregio

MODERATE

Fiachetteria Toscana. San Giovanni Crisostomo, Cannaregio 5719. ☎ **041/5-28-52-81.** Reservations recommended. Main courses 18,000L–35,000L ($10.45–$20.30). AE, DC, MC, V. Wed–Mon 12:30–2:30pm and 7:30–10:30pm. Closed July. Vaporetto: Rialto. VENETIAN.

Though this purports to be a rather stylish restaurant, there may be some rough points in the service (the staff is hysterically busy) and presentations. Nonetheless, this is the preferred choice of many food-savvy Venetians who often regard it as a venue for a celebration. Despite the high prices and the closely packed tables, this is a hot spot for trendies who appreciate the see-and-be-seen ambience, offering a vaguely permissive aura where filmmakers and models can feel comfortable. The dining rooms are on two levels, the upstairs of which is somewhat more claustrophobic. In the evening, the downstairs is especially appealing with its romantic candlelight.

Menu items include frittura della Serenissima (mixed platter of fried seafood with vegetables), veal scallops with lemon-marsala sauce and mushrooms, ravioli stuffed with whitefish and herbs, and several kinds of Tuscan-style beefsteak.

✪ **Ristorante à la Vecia Cavana.** Rio dei Terrà SS. Apostoli, Cannaregio 4624. ☎ **041/5-28-71-06.** Main courses 35,000L–60,000L ($20.30–$34.80); fixed-price menu 35,000L–100,000L ($20.30–$58). AE, DC, MC, V. Fri–Wed noon–2:30pm and 7:30–10:30pm. Vaporetto: Ca' d'Oro. SEAFOOD.

Ristorante à la Vecia Cavana is off the tourist circuit and well worth the trek through the winding streets to find it. A cavana is a place where gondolas are parked, a sort of liquid garage, and the site of this restaurant was such a place in the Middle Ages. When you enter, you'll be greeted by brick arches, stone columns, terra-cotta floors, framed modern paintings, and a photo of 19th-century fishermen relaxing after a day's work. It's an appropriate introduction to a menu specializing in seafood, like a mixed grill from the Adriatic, fried scampi, fresh sole, squid, three types of risotto (each with seafood), and a spicy zuppa di pesce (fish soup). Antipasti di pesce Cavana is an assortment of just about every sea creature. The food is authentic and seems prepared for the Venetian palate—not necessarily for the glitzy foreign visitor's.

INEXPENSIVE

✪ **Ai Tre Spiedi.** Salizzada San Cazian, Cannaregio 5906. ☎ **041/520-8035.** Main courses 16,000L–26,000L ($9–$15). MC, V. Tues–Sat noon–2:30pm and 7–9:30pm, Sun 12:30–3:30pm. Vaporetto: Rialto. VENETIAN.

Venetians bring their visiting friends here to make a good impression without breaking the bank, then swear them to secrecy. Rarely will you find as pleasant a setting and as appetizing a meal as in this casually elegant trattoria with exposed-beam ceilings and some of the most reasonably priced fresh-fish dining that'll keep meat-eaters happy as well. If you order à la carte, ask the English-speaking waiters to estimate the cost of your fish entree, since it'll typically appear priced by the *etto* (200 grams).

Il Milion. Corte Prima al Milion, Cannaregio 5841. ☎ **041/522-9302.** Reservations recommended. Main courses 20,000L–29,000L ($11.60–$16.80). No credit cards. Thurs–Tues noon–2pm and 6:30–11pm. Closed Aug. Vaporetto: Rialto. VENETIAN.

With a 300-year-old tradition of feeding patrons and a location near the rear of San Giovanni Crisostomo, this is one of Venice's oldest restaurants. It's named after the book written by Marco Polo, *Il*

Milion, describing his travels. In fact, it occupies a town house owned long ago by members of the explorer's family. The bar, incidentally, is a favorite with some of the gondoliers of Venice. Menu items include what reads like a who's who of well-recognized Venetian platters, each fresh and well prepared. Examples are veal kidneys, calves' liver with fried onions, grilled sardines, spaghetti with clams, risotto flavored with squid ink, and a fritto misto of fried fish. The staff is charming and friendly.

Tiziano Bar. Salizzada San Giovanni Cristotomo (midway between the church of San Giovanni Cristotomo and the Teatro Mulibran), Cannaregio 5747. ☎ **041/5-23-55-44.** Main dishes 8,000L–14,000L ($4.65–$8.10). No credit cards. Sun–Fri 8am–10:30pm. Vaporetto: Rialto. SANDWICHES/PASTA/PIZZA.

The Tiziano Bar is a *tavola calda* (literally "hot table"). There's no waiter service—you eat standing at a counter or on one of the high stools. The place is known in Venice for selling pizza by the yard. From noon to 3pm, it serves hot pastas like rigatoni and cannelloni. But throughout the day you can order sandwiches or perhaps a plate of mozzarella.

4 On or Near Riva degli Schiavoni

EXPENSIVE

✪ **Do Leoni.** In the Londra Palace, Riva degli Schiavoni, Castello 4171. ☎ **041/5-20-05-33.** Reservations recommended. Main courses 30,000L–60,000L ($17.40–$34.80); 3-course lunch 42,000L ($24.35) without drinks. Hotel guests receive 20% discount (excludes fixed-price menu). AE, DC, MC, V. Restaurant, daily 11:30am–3pm and 7:30–11pm; bar, daily 10am–1am. Vaporetto: San Zaccaria. VENETIAN/INTERNATIONAL.

For years, this restaurant was known by the French version of its name, Les Deux Lions. In the elegant Londra Palace, it offers a panoramic view of a 19th-century equestrian statue ringed with heroic women taming—you guessed it—lions. The restaurant is filled with scarlet and gold, a motif of lions patterned into the carpeting, and reproductions of English furniture. Lunches are brief buffet-style affairs, where patrons serve themselves from a large choice of hot and cold Italian and international food. The appealing candlelit dinners are more formal, emphasizing Venetian cuisine. The chef's undeniable skill is reflected in such dishes as chilled fish terrine, baked salmon in champagne sauce, and baby rooster with green-pepper sauce. Depending on the weather, you can dine out on the piazza overlooking the lions and their masters.

MODERATE

Ristorante Corte Sconta. Calle del Pestrin, Castello 3886. ☎ **041/5-22-70-24.** Reservations required. Main courses 20,000L–35,000L ($11.60–$20.30); fixed-price menu 70,000L–85,000L ($40.60–$49.30). AE, DC, MC, V. Tues–Sat 12:30–2:30pm and 7:30–9:30pm. Closed Jan 7–Feb 7 and July 15–Aug 15. Vaporetto: Arsenale. SEAFOOD.

Corte Sconta is behind a narrow storefront you'd probably ignore if you didn't know about this place. On a narrow alley whose name is shared by at least three other streets in Venice (this one is near Campo Bandiere e Moro and San Giovanni in Bragora), this modest restaurant has a multicolored marble floor, plain wooden tables, and no serious attempt at decoration. It has become well known, however, as a sophisticated gathering place for artists, writers, and filmmakers. As the depiction of the satyr chasing the mermaid above the entrance implies, it's a fish restaurant, serving a variety of grilled creatures (much of the "catch" is largely unknown in North America). The fresh fish is flawlessly grilled and flawlessly fresh—the gamberi, for example, is placed live on the grill. A great start is marinated salmon with arugula and pomegranate seeds in rich olive oil. If you don't like fish, a tender beef fillet is available. The big stand-up bar in an adjoining room seems to be almost a private fraternity of the locals.

INEXPENSIVE

Trattoria da Remigio. Salizzada dei Greci, Castello 3416. ☎ **041/5-23-00-89.** Reservations recommended. Pasta courses 5,000L–9,000L ($3–$5.40); main courses 8,000L–35,000L ($4.80–$21). AE, DC, MC, V. Wed–Mon 12:30–3pm; Wed–Sun 7:30–1pm. Vaporetto: San Zaccaria. ITALIAN/VENETIAN.

Famous for its straightforward renditions of Adriatic classics, Remigio is the kind of place where you can order a simple plate of gnocchi alla pescatora (homemade gnocchi in a tomato-based sauce of seafood) and know it'll be *buonissimo*. English-speaking headwaiter Pino will talk you through the day's fish dishes (John Dory, sole, monkfish, cuttlefish); sold by weight (*etto*), they're fresh and perfectly prepared, as is any antipasto. There are a dozen or so nice meat possibilities, quite a concession in this fish-crazed town. There are only two pleasant but smallish dining rooms, so even late on a winter weekday you can expect a wait unless you've reserved. Remigio's is quite well known though not easy to find, so just ask any local.

5 Castello

MODERATE

Al Covo. Campiello della Pescaria, Castello 3968. ☎ **041/522-3812.** Reservations recommended for dinner. Main courses 38,000L ($22.05); fixed-price lunch 48,000L ($27.85). AE, MC, V. Fri–Tues 12:45–2:15pm and 7:45–10:15pm. Vaporetto: Arsenale. VENETIAN/SEAFOOD.

The antique setting and sophisticated management and cookery by Cesare Benelli and his Texas-born wife, Diane, create a special charm as well as very fresh and very appealing Venetian dishes. What's their preferred dish? They respond, "That's like asking us, 'Which of your children do you prefer?' since we strongly attach ourselves to the development of each dish." Look for a succulent reinvention of a medieval version of fish soup; potato gnocchi flavored with go (a local whitefish); seafood ravioli; linguine zestly blended with zucchini and fresh peas; and delicious fritto misto with scampi, squid, a bewildering array of fish, and deep-fried vegetables like zucchini flowers. Al Covo prides itself on not having any freezers, guaranteeing that all food is imported fresh every day. As you set out for this place, be alert to the fact that it's near Piazza San Marco, not near Rialto, as is frequently thought because of a square there with a similar name.

Nuova Rivetta. Campo San Filippo, Castello 4625. ☎ **041/5-28-73-02.** Reservations required. Main courses 16,000L–28,000L ($9.30–$16.25). AE, MC, V. Tues–Sun 10am–10pm. Closed July 23–Aug 20. Vaporetto: San Zaccaria. SEAFOOD.

Nuova Rivetta is an old-fashioned trattoria where you get good food at a good price. Many find it best for lunch during a stroll around Venice. The most representative dish is frittura di pesce, a mixed fish fry from the Adriatic that includes squid or various other "sea creatures" that turned up at the day's market. Other specialties are gnocchi stuffed with Adriatic spider crab, pasticcio of fish (a main course), and spaghetti flavored with squid ink. The most typical wine is Prosecco, whose bouquet is refreshing and fruity with a slightly sharp flavor; for centuries it has been one of the most celebrated wines of the Veneto.

Ristorante al Mondo Novo. Salizzada di San Lio, Castello 5409. ☎ **041/5-20-06-98.** Reservations recommended. Main courses 15,000L–35,000L ($8.70–$20.30); fixed-price menu 23,000L–39,000L ($13.35–$22.60). AE, MC, V. Tues–Sun 11am–3pm and 7pm–midnight (last order). Vaporetto: Rialto or San Marco. VENETIAN/SEAFOOD.

In a building from the Renaissance, with a dining room outfitted in a regional style, this well-established restaurant offers professional service and a kindly staff. Plus, it stays open later than many of its nearby competitors. Menu items include a selection of seafood, prepared as frittura misto dell'Adriatico or charcoal grilled. Other items are macaroni alla verdura (with fresh vegetables and greens), an antipasti of fresh fish, and beef fillets with pepper sauce and rissole potatoes. Locals who frequent the place always order the fresh fish, knowing that the owner is a wholesaler in the Rialto fish market.

INEXPENSIVE

✪ **Alfredo, Alfredo.** Campo San Felipe e Giacomi, Castello 4294. ☎ **041/ 5-22-53-31.** Main courses 17,000L–28,000L ($9.85–$16.25); fixed-price menu 22,000L ($12.75). AE, DC, MC, V. Thurs–Tues 11am–2am. Vaporetto: San Zaccaria. VENETIAN.

Alfredo, Alfredo might be classified as a coffee shop. You can order any number of items prepared in short order, like spaghetti with a number of sauces, freshly made salads, crepes, various grilled meats, and omelets. The food isn't always first-rate and the atmosphere is a bit hysterical at times, but its long hours make it a convenient spot for a light meal at almost any time of day.

Al Mascaron. Calle Lunga Santa Maria Formosa 5225, Castello. ☎ **041/ 522-5995.** Reservations recommended. Main courses 15,000L–40,000L ($8.70–$23.20). No credit cards. Mon–Sat 12:30–3pm and 7–11pm. Vaporetto: Rialto or an Marco. VENETIAN.

Loud and unpretentious, offering three dining rooms decorated with Venetian artifacts, this is the type of restaurant that encourages patrons to sit next to strangers at long trestle tables on which are slammed copious portions. These are likely to include deep-fried calamari, spaghetti with lobster, monkfish in a salt crust, pastas, savory risottos, and Venetian-style calves' liver (which locals prefer rather pink), plus the best seafood of the day made into salads. There's also a convivial bar, where locals drop in to spread the gossip of the day, play cards, have a glass of vino, and order snacks.

Restaurant da Bruno. Calle del Paradiso, Castello 5731. ☎ **041/ 5-22-14-80.** Main courses 12,000L–25,000L ($6.95–$14.50); fixed-price menu 24,000L ($13.90). AE, DC, MC, V. Wed–Mon noon–3pm and 7–11pm. Closed 1 week in Jan. Vaporetto: San Marco or Rialto. VENETIAN.

On a narrow street about halfway between the Rialto Bridge and Piazza San Marco, this is like a country taverna and attracts its crowds by grilling meats on an open-hearth fire. You get your antipasti at the counter and watch your prosciutto order being prepared—paper-thin slices of spicy flavored ham wrapped around breadsticks (grissini). In the right season, da Bruno offers some of the finest game dishes in Venice; if featured, try its capriolo (roebuck) and its fagiano (pheasant). A typical Venetian dish prepared well here is the zuppa di pesce (fish soup). Other specialties are fillet of beef with pepper sauce, veal scaloppine with wild mushrooms, scampi and calamari, and squid with polenta. After that rich fare, you may settle for a macédoine of mixed fruit for dessert.

6 San Polo

MODERATE

❂ **Osteria da Fiore.** Calle del Scaletèr, San Polo 2202. ☎ **041/72-13-08.** Reservations required. Main courses 36,000L–42,000L ($20.90–$24.35). AE, DC, MC, V. Tues–Sat 12:30–2:30pm and 8–10:30pm. Closed 3 weeks in Aug and Dec 25–Jan 14. Vaporetto: San Tomà. SEAFOOD.

The breath of the Adriatic seems to blow through this place, though how the wind finds this little restaurant tucked away in a labyrinth is a mystery. An imaginative, changing fare is offered, depending on the availability of fresh fish and produce. If you have a love of maritime foods, you'll find everything from scampi (a sweet Adriatic prawn, cooked in as many ways as there are chefs) to granzeola, a type of spider crab. In days gone by, we've sampled fried calamari (cuttlefish), risotto with scampi, tagliata with rosemary, masenette (tiny green crabs you eat shell and all), and canoce (mantis shrimp). For your wine, we suggest Prosecco, which has a distinctive golden-yellow color and a bouquet that's refreshing and fruity. The proprietors extend a hearty welcome to match their fare.

Poste Vecchie. Pescheria Rialto, San Polo 1608. ☎ **041/72-18-22.** Reservations recommended. Main courses 21,000L–45,000L ($12.20–$26.10). AE, DC, MC, V. Wed–Mon noon–3:30pm and 7–10:30pm. Vaporetto: Rialto. SEAFOOD.

This charming restaurant is near the Rialto fish market and connected to the rest of the city by a small privately owned bridge. It opened in the early 1500s as a post office—when they used to serve food to fortify the mail carriers for their deliveries. Today it's the oldest restaurant in Venice, with a pair of intimate dining rooms (both graced with paneling, murals, and 16th-century mantelpieces) and a courtyard that evokes the countryside. Menu items include superfresh fish from the nearby markets; a salad of shellfish and exotic mushrooms; tagliolini flavored with squid ink, crabmeat, and fish sauce; and the pièce de résistance, seppie (cuttlefish) à la veneziana with polenta. If you don't like fish, calves' liver or veal shank with ham and cheese are also well prepared. The desserts come rolling to your table on a trolley and are usually delicious.

Trattoria Antica Besseta. Calle della Savia, San Polo 1395. ☎ **041/72-16-87.** Reservations required. Main courses 30,000L–35,000L ($17.40–$20.30). AE, MC, V. Thurs–Mon 12:30–2:30pm and 7:30–10:30pm. Closed Aug 1–15. Vaporetto: Rive di Biasio. VENETIAN.

If you manage to find the place (go with a good map), you'll be rewarded with true Venetian cuisine at its most unpretentious. Head for Campo San Giacomo dell'Orio, then negotiate your way across infrequently visited piazzas and winding alleys. Push through saloon doors into a bar area filled with modern art. The dining room in back is ringed with paintings and illuminated with wagon-wheel chandeliers. Nereo Volpe and his wife, Mariuccia, and one of their sons are the guiding force, the chefs, the buyers, and even the "talking menus." The food depends on what looked good in the market that morning, so the menu could include roast chicken, fried scampi, fritto misto, spaghetti in sardine sauce, various roasts, and a selection from the day's catch. The Volpe family produces two kinds of their own wine, a Pinot Blanc and a Cabernet.

INEXPENSIVE

✪ **Pizzeria alle Oche.** Calle del Tintor, San Polo 1552B. ☎ **041/524-1161.** Reservations not necessary. Pizzas 6,500L–14,000L ($3.90–$8.40); main courses 10,000L–22,000L ($6–$13.20). MC, V. Daily noon–3pm and 7pm–midnight. Closed Mon Oct–Mar. Vaporetto: San Stae. ITALIAN.

In an antique building 2 blocks south of San Giacomo dell'Orio, you'll find this pleasant restaurant where no one will mind if you order from a menu listing 85 kinds of pizza. The most popular are pizza capricciosa (with prosciutto, mushrooms, and artichoke hearts), pizza ai quattro formaggio (with four kinds of cheeses), and pizza alle Diavolo (with red hot peppers). More outlandish and better suited just for conversation's sake, is a rarely sold pizza with pears or pineapple. There's also a selection of fresh fish that tastes best when grilled and a well-seasoned array of steaks, veal, chicken, and vegetarian dishes. During clement weather, a handful of tables are set on the sidewalk in front. *Warning:* You should be prepared to wait, for this once closely guarded secret is a secret no more.

✪ **Trattoria alla Madonna.** Calle della Madonna, San Polo 594. ☎ **041/ 5-22-38-24.** Reservations recommended but not always accepted. Main courses 18,000–22,000L ($10.45–$12.75). AE, MC, V. Thurs–Tues noon–3pm and 7:15–10pm. Closed Jan 7–Feb 7 and Aug 1–15. Vaporetto: Rialto. VENETIAN.

No, this place has nothing to do with *that* Madonna. It opened in 1954 in a 300-year-old building near the Rialto Bridge, and is one of Venice's most popular and characteristic trattorie, specializing in traditional Venetian recipes and grilled fresh fish. A good beginning might be the antipasto frutti di mare (fresh seafood). Pastas, polentas, risottos, meats (including fegato alla veneziana, liver with onions), and many kinds of irreproachably fresh fish are widely available.

Many creatures of the sea are displayed in a refrigerated case near the entrance.

7   Dorsoduro

MODERATE

La Furatola. Calle Lunga San Barnaba, Dorsoduro 2870A. ☎ **041/ 5-20-85-94.** Reservations recommended for dinner. Main courses 25,000L– 45,000L ($14.50–$26.10). AE, DC, MC, V. Fri–Tues noon–2:30pm and 7– 10:30pm. Closed July–Aug. Vaporetto: Ca' Rezzonico or Accademia. SEAFOOD.

La Furatola (an old Venetian word meaning "restaurant") is very much a Dorsoduro neighborhood hangout, but it has captured the imagination of local foodies. It occupies a 300-year-old building, along a narrow flagstone-paved street you'll need a good map and a lot of patience to find. Perhaps you'll have lunch here after a visit to San Rocco, only a short distance away. In the simple dining room, the specialty is fish brought to your table in a wicker basket so you can judge its size and freshness by its bright eyes and red gills. A display of seafood antipasti is set out near the entrance. A standout is the baby octopus boiled and eaten with a drop of red-wine vinegar. Eel comes with a medley of mixed fried fish, including baby cuttlefish, prawns, and squid rings.

✪ **Locanda Montin.** Fondamenta di Borgo, Dorsoduro 1147. ☎ **041/ 5-22-71-51.** Reservations recommended. Main courses 20,000L–30,000L ($11.60–$17.40). AE, DC, MC, V. Tues 12:30–2:30pm, Thurs–Mon 12:30– 2:30pm and 7:30–9:30pm. Vaporetto: Accademia. INTERNATIONAL/ITALIAN.

The Montin is the kind of rapidly disappearing inn that nearly every literary and artistic figure in Venice has visited since it opened just after World War II. Famous patrons have included Ezra Pound, Jackson Pollock, Mark Rothko, and many of the artist friends of the late Peggy Guggenheim. It's owned and run by the Carretins, who have covered the walls with paintings donated by or bought from their many friends and guests. The arbor-covered garden courtyard of this 17th-century building is filled with regulars, many of whom allow their favorite waiter to select most of the items for their meal. The frequently changing menu includes a variety of salads, grilled meats, and fish caught in the Adriatic. Dessert might be semifreddo di fragoline, a tempting chilled liqueur-soaked cake, capped with whipped cream and wild strawberries.

INEXPENSIVE

Linea d'Ombra. Fondamente delle Zattere, Dorsoduro 19. ☎ **041/ 528-5259.** Reservations not necessary. Main courses 30,000L–50,000L

($17.40–$29). AE, DC, MC, V. Thurs–Tues noon–3:30pm and Thurs–Sat and Mon–Tues 7:30–10:30pm. Vaporetto: Salute. VENETIAN.

This popular bar/pub that spills onto a panoramic terrace during clement weather doubles as an informal trattoria featuring traditional recipes. You can order dishes that include Venetian-style risotto with octopus and squid ink; Venetian-style calves' liver; a wide selection of fish; piquant grilled scampi; and the most popular pasta in Venice, *bigoli in salsa*. The inspiration for the name of this restaurant derives from the fascination of a former owner for Joseph Conrad's novella *The Shadow Line*.

✪ **Ristorante alle Zattere.** Fondamenta Zattere ai Gesuati, Dorsoduro 795. ☎ 041/520-4224. Reservations recommended. Main courses 22,000L–35,000L ($13.20–$21). MC, V. Wed–Mon noon–3:30pm and 7–11pm. Closed Nov. Vaporetto: Zattere. VENETIAN.

To get here, you'll have to walk to a point near the southernmost embankment of the Dorsoduro neighborhood, just east of the Chiesa dei Gesuati. In this thick-walled antique house, you'll find good food and a sweeping terrace overlooking one of the busiest waterways in the city. In fact, many diners come here just for the view, as it's one of the few restaurants with a terrace overlooking the Canal della Giudecca. Sit back on a summer night while devouring a meal and take time to watch the passing parade that looks more like a Hollywood film than reality, with its rowboats, gondolas, vaporetti, and cruise ships.

8   Isola della Giudecca

VERY EXPENSIVE

✪ **Ristorante Cipriani.** In the Hotel Cipriani, Isola della Giudecca 10. ☎ 041/5-20-77-44. Reservations required. Main courses 23,000L–66,000L ($13.35–$38.30). AE, DC, MC, V. Daily 12:30–3pm and 8–10:30pm. Closed Nov–Mar. Vaporetto: Zitelle. INTERNATIONAL.

The grandest of the hotel restaurants, the Cipriani offers a sublime but relatively simple cuisine, depending on the freshest of ingredients perfectly prepared by one of the best-trained staffs along the Adriatic. This isn't a family place: Children under 6 aren't allowed. You can dine in the more formal room with Murano chandeliers and Fortuny curtains when the weather is nippy or out on the extensive terrace overlooking the lagoon. Freshly made pasta is a specialty, and it's among the finest we've ever sampled. Try the taglierini verdi with noodles and ham au gratin. Chef's specialties include mixed fried scampi and squid with tender vegetables and sautéed veal fillets with spring artichokes. Come here in October for the last Bellinis of the white peach season and the first white truffles of the season served in a champagne risotto.

EXPENSIVE

✪ **Harry's Dolci.** Fondamenta San Biago 773, Isola della Giudecca. ☎ **041/5-20-83-37.** Reservations recommended, especially Sat–Sun. Main courses 30,000L–40,000L ($17.40–$23.20); fixed-price menu 75,000L ($43.50). AE, MC, V. Wed–Mon noon–3pm and 7–10:30pm. Closed Nov–Mar 30. Vaporetto: S. Eufemia. INTERNATIONAL/ITALIAN.

The people at the famed Harry's Bar have established their latest enclave far from the maddening crowds of Piazza Sam Marco on this little-visited island. From the quay-side windows of this chic place, you can watch seagoing vessels, including everything from yachts to lagoon-based barges. White napery and uniformed waiters grace a modern room, where no one minds if you order only coffee and ice cream or perhaps a selection from the large pastry menu (the zabaglione cake is divine). Popular items are carpaccio Cipriani, chicken salad, club sandwiches, gnocchi, and house-style cannelloni. Dishes are deliberately kept simple, but each is well prepared.

9 The Lido

MODERATE

Favorita. Via Francesco Duodo 33, Lido di Venezia. ☎ **041/526-1626.** Main courses 23,000L–70,000L ($13.35–$40.60). AE, DC, MC, V. Tues–Sun 12:30–2:30pm and 7:30–10:30pm. Vaporetto: Lido di Venezia. SEAFOOD.

Occupying two dining rooms and a garden that has thrived here since the 1920s, this place was reputedly named after Gabriella, wife (and presumably "the favorite") of Vittorio Emanuele, who occasionally stopped in for refreshment during her stops on the Lido. It's operated by the Pradel family, now in their third generation of ownership. Their years of experience contribute to flavorful, impeccably prepared seafood and shellfish, many of them grilled, served in the rustically beamed interior or at tables amid the flowering vines of the garden. Try the trenette (spaghetti-like pasta) with baby squid and eggplant; potato-based gnocchi with crabs from the Venetian lagoon; and grilled versions of virtually every fish in the Adriatic, including eel, sea bass, turbot, and sole.

Ristorante Belvedere. Piazzale Santa Maria Elisabetta 4, Lido di Venezia. ☎ **041/5-26-01-15.** Reservations required. Main courses 12,000L–50,000L ($6.95–$29); fixed-price menu 33,000L ($19.15). AE, DC, MC, V. Tues–Sun noon–2:30pm and 7–9:30pm. Closed Nov 4 to mid-Feb. Vaporetto: Lido. VENETIAN.

Outside the big hotels, the best food on the Lido is served at the Belvedere. Don't be put off by its location, across from where the vaporetto from Venice stops. In such a location, you might expect a touristy place. Actually, the Belvedere attracts some of the finest people of Venice. They often come here as an excursion, knowing they can get some of the best fish along the Adriatic. Tables are placed outside, and there's a glass-enclosed portion for windy days. The main dining room is attractive, with cane-backed bentwood chairs and big windows. In back, reached through a separate entrance, is a busy cafe. Main dishes include the chef's special sea bass, along with grilled dorade (or sole), and fried scampi. You might begin with the special fish antipasti or spaghetti en papillote (cooked in parchment).

6

Exploring Venice

*V*enice appears to have been created specifically to entertain its legions of callers. Ever since the body of St. Mark was smuggled out of Alexandria and entombed in the basilica, Venice has been host to a never-ending stream of visitors—famous, infamous, and otherwise—from all over the world.

Venice has perpetually captured the imagination of poets, artists, and travelers. Wordsworth, Byron, and Shelley addressed poems to the city, and it has been written about or used as a setting by many contemporary writers.

In the pages ahead, we'll explore the city's great art and architecture. But, unlike Florence, Venice would reward its guests with treasures even if they never ducked inside a museum or church. In the city on the islands, the frame eternally competes with the picture inside.

"For all its vanity and villainy," wrote Lewis Mumford, "life touched some of its highest moments in Venice."

1 Piazza San Marco

✪ **Piazza San Marco (St. Mark's Square)** was the heartbeat of La Serenissima in the heyday of its glory as a seafaring republic, the crystallization of the city's dreams and aspirations. If you have only a day for Venice, you need not leave the square, as the city's major attractions, like the Basilica of St. Mark and the Doge's Palace, are centered here or nearby.

The traffic-free square is frequented by visitors and pigeons and sometimes even by Venetians. If you rise at dawn, you can almost have the piazza to yourself, and as you watch the sun come up, the sheen of gold mosaics glistens with a mystical beauty. At around 9am, the overstuffed pigeons are fed by the city (if you're caught under the whir, you'll think you're witnessing a remake of Hitchcock's *The Birds*). At mid-afternoon the tourists reign supreme, and it's not surprising in July to witness a scuffle over a camera angle. At sunset, when the two Moors in the Clock Tower strike the

Venice Attractions

 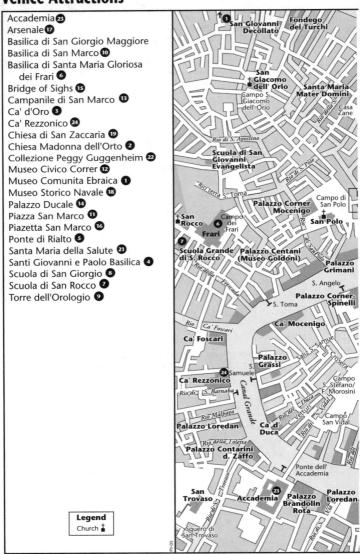
Legend

Church ⛪

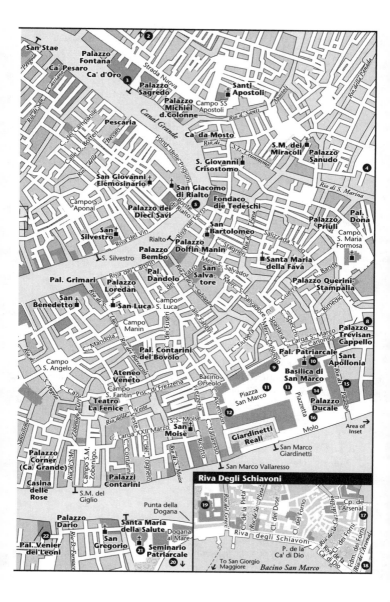

San Stae

Palazzo Fontana

Ca' Pesaro

Ca' d'Oro

Palazzo Sagredo

Palazzo Michiel d.Colonne

Campo SS Apostoli

Santi Apostoli

Strada Nuova

Canal Grande

Pescaria

Fond. delle Prioli

Ca' da-Mosto

Rio di

S.M. dei Miracoli

Palazzo Sanudo

S. Giovanni Crisostomo

San Giovanni Elemosinario

San Giacomo di Rialto

Fondaco die Tedeschi

Palazzo Priuli

Campo S. Aponal

Palazzo dei Dieci Savi

Rialto

San Silvestro

Riva del Vin

San Bartolomeo

Salizzada S. Lio

Santa Maria della Fava

Campo S. Maria Formosa

Pal. Dona

S. Silvestro

Rialto

Palazzo Bembo

Palazzo Dolfin-Manin

San Salvatore

Palazzo Querini Stampalia

Pal. Grimani

Palazzo Loredan

Pal. Dandolo

San Benedetto

San Luca

Campo S. Luca

Campo Manin

Palazzo Trevisan Cappello

Pal. Contarini del Bovolo

Campo S. Angelo

Ateneo Veneto

Pal. Patriarcale

Sant Apollonia

Teatro La Fenice

Bacino Orseolo

Basilica di San Marco

Piazza San Marco

Giardinetti Reali

San Moise

Palazzo Ducale

Piazzetta

Molo

Area of Inset

San Marco Giardinetti

San Marco Vallaresso

Palazzo Corner (Ca' Grande)

Casina delle Rose

Palazzi Contarini

S.M. del Giglio

Punta della Dogana

Palazzo Dario

Santa Maria della Salute

San Gregorio

Dogana al Mare

Pal. Venier dei Leoni

Seminario Patriarcale

Riva Degli Schiavoni

Rio del Greci

Rio de la Pieta

Ct. del Dose

Ct. del Forno

Cp. de l'Arsenal

Riva degli Schiavoni

P. de la Ca' di Dio

To San Giorgio Maggiore

Bacino San Marco

79

end of another day, lonely sailors begin a usually frustrated search for those hot spots that characterized the Venice of yore. Deeper into the evening, the strollers parade by or stop for an espresso at the fashionable Caffè Florian and sip while listening to a band concert.

Thanks to Napoléon, the square was unified architecturally. The emperor added the Fabbrica Nuova facing the basilica, thus bridging the Old and New Procuratie on either side. Flanked with medieval-looking palaces, Sansovino's Library, elegant shops, and colonnades, the square is now finished—unlike Piazza della Signoria in Florence.

If Piazza San Marco is Europe's drawing room, then the piazza's satellite, **Piazzetta San Marco,** is Europe's antechamber. Hedged in by the Doge's Palace, Sansovino's Library, and a side of St. Mark's, the tiny square faces the Grand Canal. Two tall granite columns grace the square. One is surmounted by a winged lion, representing St. Mark. The other is topped by a statue of a man taming a dragon, supposedly the dethroned patron saint Theodore. Both columns came from the East in the 12th century.

During Venice's heyday, dozens of victims either lost their heads or were strung up here, many of them first being subjected to torture that would've made the Marquis de Sade flinch. One, for example, had his teeth hammered in, his eyes gouged out, and his hands cut off before being strung up. Venetian justice became notorious throughout Europe. If you stand with your back to the canal, looking toward the south facade of St. Mark's, you'll see the so-called *Virgin and Child* of the poor baker, a mosaic honoring Pietro Fasiol (also Faziol), a young man unjustly sentenced to death on a charge of murder.

To the left of the entrance to the Doge's Palace are four porphyry figures, which, for want of a better description, the Venetians called "Moors." These puce-colored fellows are huddled close together, as if afraid. Considering the decapitations and tortures that have occurred on the piazzetta, it's no wonder.

A St. Mark's Warning

A dress code for men and women prohibiting shorts, bare arms and shoulders, and skirts above the knee is strictly enforced at all times in the basilica. You *will* be turned away. In addition, you must remain silent and cannot take photographs.

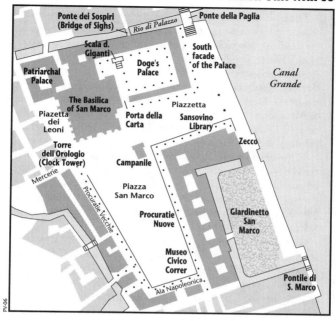

For a detailed stroll of the piazza, the basilica, and the Doge's Palace, see the first walking tour in chapter 7.

✪ **Basilica di San Marco (St. Mark's Basilica).** Piazza San Marco. ☎ **041/5-22-52-05.** Basilica and baptistery free; treasury 4,000L ($2.30); presbytery 3,000L ($1.75); Marciano Museum 3,000L ($1.75). Basilica, baptistery, and presbytery Apr–Sept Mon–Sat 9:30am–5:30pm; Oct–Mar Mon–Sat 9:30am–5pm, Sun 1:30–4:30pm. Treasury Mon–Sat 9:30am–5pm, Sun 2–5pm. Marciano Museum Apr–Sept Mon–Sat 10am–5:30pm, Sun 2–4:30pm; Oct–Mar Mon–Sat 10am–4:45pm, Sun 2–4:30pm. Vaporetto: San Marco.

Dominating Piazza San Marco is the "Church of Gold," one of the world's greatest and most richly embellished churches. In fact, it looks as if it had been moved intact from Istanbul. The basilica is a conglomeration of styles, though it's particularly indebted to Byzantine. Like Venice, St. Mark's is adorned with booty from every corner of the city's once far-flung mercantile empire—capitals from Sicily, columns from Alexandria, porphyry from Syria, and sculpture from old Constantinople.

The basilica is capped by a dome that, like a spider plant, sends off shoots, in this case a quartet of smaller-scale cupolas. Spanning the facade is a loggia, surmounted by replicas of the four famous St. Mark's horses, the *Triumphal Quadriga*. The facade's rich marble slabs and mosaics depict scenes from the lives of Jesus and St. Mark. One of the mosaics re-creates the entry of the evangelist's body into Venice: St. Mark's body, hidden in a pork barrel, was smuggled out of Alexandria in 828 and shipped to Venice. The evangelist de-throned Theodore, the Greek saint who up until then had been the patron of the city that had outgrown him.

In the **atrium** are six cupolas with mosaics illustrating scenes from the Old Testament, including the story of the Tower of Babel. The interior of the basilica, once the private chapel and pantheon of the doges, is a stunning wonderland of marbles, alabaster, porphyry, and pillars. You'll walk in awe across the undulating multicolored ocean floor, patterned with mosaics.

To the right is the **baptistery,** dominated by the Sansovino-inspired baptismal font, upon which John the Baptist is ready to pour water. If you look back at the aperture over the entry, you can see a mosaic of the dance of Salome in front of Herod and his court. Salome, wearing a star-studded russet-red dress and three white fox tails, is dancing under a platter holding John the Baptist's head. Her glassy face is that of a Madonna, not an enchantress.

After touring the baptistery, proceed up the right nave to the doorway to the oft-looted **treasury** (*tesoro*). Here you'll find the in-evitable skulls and bones of some ecclesiastical authorities under glass, plus goblets, chalices, and Gothic candelabra. The entrance to the **presbytery** is nearby. In it, on the high altar, the alleged sar-cophagus of St. Mark rests under a green marble blanket and is held by four sculptured Corinthian-style alabaster columns. The Byzantine-style **Pala d'Oro,** from Constantinople, is the rarest treasure at St. Mark's—made of gold and studded with precious stones.

On leaving the basilica, head up the stairs in the atrium to the **Marciano Museum** and the **Loggia dei Cavalli.** The star of the museum is the world-famous *Triumphal Quadriga,* four horses looted from Constantinople by Venetian crusaders during the sack of that city in 1204. These horses once surmounted the basilica but were removed because of pollution damage. This is the only *quadriga* (which means a quartet of horses yoked together) to have survived from the classical era, believed to have been cast in the 4th century. Napoléon once carted these much-traveled horses off to Paris for the Arc de Triomphe du Carrousel, but they were returned to Venice in 1815. The museum, with its mosaics and tapestries, is especially interesting, but also be sure to walk out onto the loggia for a view of Piazza San Marco.

Campanile di San Marco (Bell Tower of San Marco). Piazza San Marco. ☎ **041/5-22-40-64.** Admission 8,000L ($4.65) adults, 3,000L ($1.75) children. May–Oct daily 9am–8pm; Nov–Apr daily 9:30am–3:45pm. Vaporetto: San Marco.

One summer night in 1902, the bell tower of St. Mark's, suffering from years of rheumatism in the damp Venetian climate, gave out a warning sound that sent the fashionable coffee drinkers in the piazza scurrying for their lives. But the campanile gracefully waited until the next morning, July 14, before tumbling into the piazza. The Venetians rebuilt their belfry, and it's now safe to climb to the top. However, unlike Italy's other bell towers, where you have to brave narrow, steep spiral staircases to reach the top, here you can take an elevator to get a pigeon's view of the city. It's a particularly good vantage point for viewing the cupolas of the basilica.

Torre dell'Orologio (Clock Tower). Piazza San Marco. ☎ **041/5-23-18-79.** Vaporetto: San Marco.

The two Moors striking the bell atop this clock tower, soaring over the Old Procuratie, represent one of the most characteristic Venetian scenes. The clock under the winged lion not only tells the time but also is a boon to the astrologer: It matches the signs of the zodiac with the position of the sun. If the movement of the Moors striking the hour seems slow in today's fast-paced world, remember how many centuries the poor wretches have been at their task without time off. The "Moors" originally represented two European shepherds, but after having been reproduced in bronze, they've grown darker with the passing of time. As a consequence, they came to be called Moors by the Venetians.

The tower is currently being restored, under the technical expertise of Piaget, the Geneva-based watchmaker. Repairs are slated for completion in spring 1999. Alas, even after the restoration, visitors will probably not be allowed inside the tower. Authorities have decided that interior visits are dangerous, and you can view the tower only from the outside.

✪ **Palazzo Ducale and the Ponte dei Sospiri (Ducal Palace and the Bridge of Sighs).** Piazzetta San Marco. ☎ **041/5-22-49-51.** Admission (including admission to Museo Civico Correr) 17,000L ($9.85) adults, 10,000L ($5.80) students with ID, 6,000L ($3.50) children 6–13; free children 5 and under. Apr–Oct daily 9am–7pm; Nov–Mar daily 9am–5pm. Vaporetto: San Marco.

You enter the Palace of the Doges through the magnificent 15th-century **Porta della Carta** at the piazzetta. This Venetian Gothic palazzo gleams in the tremulous light somewhat like a frosty birthday cake in pinkish red marble and white Istrian stone. Italy's grandest civic structure, it dates from 1309, though a 1577 fire destroyed much of the original. That fire made ashes of many of the palace's greatest masterpieces and almost spelled doom for the building itself, as the new post-Renaissance architectural fervor was in the air. However, sanity prevailed. Many of the greatest Venetian painters of the 16th century contributed to the restored palace, replacing the canvases or frescoes of the older masters.

If you enter from the piazzetta, past the four porphyry Moors, you'll be in the splendid Renaissance courtyard, one of the most recent additions to a palace that has benefited from the work of many architects with widely varying tastes. You can take the "giants' stairway" to the upper loggia—so called because of the two Sansovino statues of mythological figures.

After climbing the Sansovino stairway of gold you'll enter some get-acquainted rooms. Proceed to the **Sala di Antecollegio,** housing the palace's greatest works—notably Veronese's *Rape of Europa,* to the far left on the right wall. Tintoretto is well represented with his *Three Graces* and his *Bacchus and Ariadne.* Some critics consider the latter his supreme achievement. The ceiling in the adjoining **Sala del Collegio** bears allegorical paintings by Veronese. As you proceed to the right, you'll enter the **Sala del Senato o Pregadi,** with its allegorical painting by Tintoretto in the center of the ceiling.

It was in the **Sala del Consiglio dei Dieci,** with its gloomy paintings, that the dreaded Council of Ten (often called the Terrible Ten for good reason) used to assemble to decide who was in need of decapitation. In the antechamber, bills of accusation were dropped in the lion's mouth.

The excitement continues downstairs. You can wander through the once-private apartments of the doges to the grand **Sala del Maggior Consiglio,** with Veronese's allegorical *Triumph of Venice* on the ceiling. The most outstanding feature, however, is Tintoretto's *Paradise,* over the Grand Council chamber—said to be the world's largest oil painting. Paradise seems to have an overpopulation problem, perhaps reflecting Tintoretto's too-optimistic point of view (he was in his 70s when he began this monumental work and died 6 years later). The second grandiose hall, which you enter from the grand chamber, is the **Sala dello Scrutinio,** with paintings telling of Venice's past glories.

Reentering the Maggior Consiglio, follow the arrows on their trail across the **Bridge of Sighs (Ponte dei Sospiri),** linking the Doge's Palace with the Palazzo delle Prigioni. Here you'll see the cell blocks that once lodged the prisoners who felt the quick justice of the Terrible Ten. The "sighs" in the bridge's name stem from the sad laments of the numerous victims forced across it to face certain torture and possible death. The cells are somber remnants of the horror of medieval justice.

2 More Attractions

THE GRAND CANAL

Peoria may have its Main Street, Paris its Champs-Elysées, New York City its Fifth Avenue—but Venice, for uniqueness, tops them all with its ✪ **Canal Grande (Grand Canal).** Lined with palazzi (many in the Venetian Gothic style), this great road of water is filled with vaporetti, motorboats, and gondolas. The boat moorings are like peppermint sticks. The canal begins at Piazzetta San Marco on one side and Longhena's Salute Church opposite. At midpoint it's spanned by the Rialto Bridge. Eventually, the canal winds its serpentine course to the rail station.

Some of the most impressive buildings along the Grand Canal have been converted into galleries and museums. Others have been turned into cooperative apartments, but often the lower floors are now deserted. Venetian housewives aren't as incurably romantic as foreign visitors. A practical lot, these women can be seen stringing up their laundry in front of thousands of tourists.

On one foggy day, Amandine Lucie Aurore Dudevant—otherwise known as George Sand—and her effete young lover, poet Alfred de Musset, arrived via this canal. John Ruskin debunked and exposed it in *The Stones of Venice*. Robert Browning, burned out from the loss of his beloved Elizabeth and his later rejection at the hands of Lady Ashburton, settled down in a palazzo here, in which he eventually died. Eleonora Duse came this way with the young poet to whom she had given her heart, Gabriele d'Annunzio. Even Shakespeare came here in his fantasies. Intrepid guides will point out the "Palazzo de Desdemona."

The best way to see the Grand Canal is to board vaporetto no. 1 (push, shove, and gouge until you secure a seat at the front of the vessel). Settle yourself in, make sure you have your long-distance viewing glasses, and prepare yourself for a view that has thrilled even the hard-to-impress Ernest Hemingway, as well as millions of other visitors down through the ages.

Did You Know?

The Lido, the bathing beach of Venice, was the original *lido* that lent its name to innumerable bathing spots and cinemas the world over.

THE LIDO

Along the white sands of the ✪ **Lido** strolled Eleonora Duse and Gabriele d'Annunzio (*Flame of Life*), Goethe in Faustian gloom, a clubfooted Byron trying to decide with whom he was in love that day, Alfred de Musset pondering the fickle ways of George Sand, Thomas Mann's Gustave von Aschenbach with his eye on Tadzio in *Death in Venice,* and Evelyn Waugh's Sebastian Flyte and Charles Ryder with their eyes on each other in *Brideshead Revisited.* But gone is the relative isolation of yore. The de Mussets of today aren't mooning over lost loves—they're out chasing bikini-clad new ones.

Near the turn of the century, the Lido began to blossom into a fashionable beachfront resort, complete with deluxe hotels and its Casino Municipale (see chapter 9, "Venice After Dark"). However, as at other beachfront resorts throughout the world, you'll find that Lido prices are usually stratospheric.

The Lido is past its heyday. The chic of the world still patronize the Excelsior Palace and Hotel des Bains, but the beach strip is overrun with tourists and opens onto polluted waters. It's not just the beaches around Venice that are polluted but reputedly the entire Adriatic. For swimming, guests use the pools of their hotels instead. They can, however, still enjoy the Lido sands.

Even if you aren't planning to stay in this area, you should still come over and explore for an afternoon. If you don't want to tread on the beachfront property of the rarefied hotels (which have huts lining the beach like those of some tropical paradise), you can try the **Lungomare G. d'Annunzio (Public Bathing Beach)** at the end of the Gran Viale (Piazzale Ettore Sorger), a long stroll from the vaporetto stop. You can book cabins (*camerini*) and enjoy the sand. Rates change seasonally.

To reach the Lido, take vaporetto no. 1, 6, 52, or 82 (the ride takes about 15 minutes). The boat departs from a landing stage near the Doge's Palace.

3 Museums & Galleries

✪ **Galleria dell'Accademia (Academy Gallery).** Campo della Carità, Dorsoduro. ☎ **041/5-22-22-47.** Admission 12,000L ($6.95) adults; free for

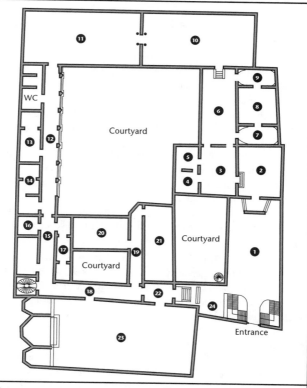

1. Venetian painters: 14th century
2. Giovanni Bellini and
   Cima da Conegliano
3. Late 15th century to
   early 16th century
4. Italian painters: 15th century
5. Giovanni Bellini and Giorgione
6. 16th century
7. Lorenzo Lotto and Salvodo
8. Palma the Elder
9. 16th-century schools of painting
10. Titian, Veronese, and Tintoretto
11. Veronese, Tintoretto, and Tiepolo
12. 18th-century landscape painters
13. Tintoretto and Bassano
14. Renovators of the 17th century
15. Minor painters of the
    18th century
16. Giambattista Piazzetta
17. Longhi, Canaletto, Carriera,
    and Guardi
18. 18th-century painters and
    engravers
19. 15th-century painters
20. Gentile Bellini and Vittorio
    Carpaccio
21. Vittorio Carpaccio
22. Bookshop
23. Venetian painters: 15th century
24. Albergo Room and Titian

A City of Art

Venice is a city of art. The adornment of its churches, its palazzi, and its public buildings is unmatched anywhere. Among this wealth of art, four important painters stand out.

Giovanni Bellini (1430–1516)   Giovanni was the most important of a family of painters that included his father, Jacopo (1400–70) and his brother Gentile (1429–1504). His work paved the way for the later innovations of Georgione and Titian. He painted religious and mythological subjects, and was a supreme portraitist. He worked in oils rather than the more common tempura, and is known for his luminous color and the harmony of his compositions. The figures in his paintings are real people—light and color bind them to his atmospheric landscapes in a harmonious whole. Giovanni's works can be seen in the Accademia and in the San Zaccaria and Frari churches. Gentile excelled in crowd scenes and panoramas; several of his paintings are in the Accademia.

Titian (1485–1576)   Tiziano Vecellio, known as Titian, came to Venice while still an adolescent to study in the workshop of Giovanni Bellini. The foremost painter of the Venetian Renaissance and a cosmopolitan man of the world, he socialized with leading academics, writers, and aristocrats of his time. Among his patrons were kings, popes, and emperors. His portraits were prized for their technical mastery and psychological perception; he painted Pope Paul III, Phillip II of Spain, and Francis I of France. As a result, much of his most important work is in museums and collections outside Italy. The work you should not miss is his *Assumption* in the Frari church. In this picture, the Virgin seems to ascend toward the heights of the apse, surrounded by soaring Gothic tracery windows that flood the space with light. This revolutionary altarpiece (1516–18), filled with movement and drama, was Titian's first major public commission and sent his reputation soaring. As Titian grew older his style of painting became increasingly broad and complex, and he was said to paint more with

children 17 and under and seniors 60 and over. Mon–Sat 9am–7pm, Sun 9am–2pm. Vaporetto: Accademia.

The glory that was Venice lives on in this remarkable collection of paintings spanning the 13th to the 18th centuries. The hallmark of the Venetian school is color and more color. From Giorgione to his fingers than with the brush. He lived to a great age, and may have been close to 100 years old at the time of his death.

Tintoretto (1518–94) Jacobo Robusti, known as Tintoretto, came from a humble background (his father was a dyer). Unlike Titian, Tintoretto was an unworldly man who traveled beyond Venice only once in his life. Devout, totally absorbed in painting religious subjects, Tintoretto rebelled against traditional representations and re-created religious scenes from new perspectives, working at a furious pace with fluid brushstrokes. His canvasses are filled with phantasmagoric light and intense, mystical spirituality. Tintoretto's principal assistants were his two sons and his daughter, Marietta Robusti, whose work can possibly be detected in a few of her father's paintings. Tintoretto is only sparsely represented in museums and collections outside Venice. His paintings are seen in churches and *scuole* (guild houses or fraternities) throughout his home city, particularly the Scuola Grande di San Rocco. Tintoretto also filled the walls of his parish church, the Madonna dell'Orto, with his dynamic, visionary canvases.

Veronese (1528–88) Paolo Calieri, as his name of Il Veronese tells us, was not born in Venice. He came to Venice from Verona in 1555, where his talent was quickly recognized. His paintings are characterized by splendor of color and are crowded with figures arranged in sinuous patterns. He painted landscapes and mythological scenes, and is especially known for his religious feast paintings. In the latter, his approach was to use lavish accessories, fashionable figures, and other secular devices. In 1573 when he was called before the Inquisition to explain the "indecent" content of his *Last Supper,* he valiantly defended his use of artistic license. Ordered to alter the work, he took the pragmatic way out and simply changed the name of the painting to *The Banquet in the House of Levi.* He is a supreme decorator, as can be seen in the Doge's Palace and the church of San Sebastiano.

Veronese, from Titian to Tintoretto to Tiepolo, the Accademia has examples of its most famous sons—often their best work. We highlight only some of the most renowned masterpieces for the first-timer in a rush.

The work of Paolo and Lorenzo Veneziano bridges the gap between Byzantine art and the beginning of a truly Venetian school of painting. See Paolo's *Coronation of the Virgin* and Lorenzo's *Annunciation*. Giovanni Bellini also loved color, but his are the harmoniously blended tints of the real world lit by real light. In his *San Giobbe Altarpiece*, each figure is individualized, dignified and serene. His Madonnas and bambini are the focus of an entire room. None but a major artist could stand the test of a salon filled with the same subject, but under Bellini's brush each Virgin achieves her individual spirituality.

Giorgione's *Tempest* is perhaps the single most famous painting at the Accademia. It is a hauntingly inexplicable juxtaposition of a man with a staff and a nude woman nursing an infant in the foreground, with a stormy view of Castelfranco, the artist's hometown, in the distance. Giorgione's colors are simple and rich, and emerge from darker and mysterious shadows. This may be the first painting with no other significance than what is shown—a poetic reverie that has tempted many to analyze it for a symbolic or allegorical message.

A most unusual *Madonna and Child* is by Cosmé Tura, the master of Ferrara, who could always be counted on to give a new twist to an old subject.

Two important works with secular themes are Mantegna's armored *St. George*, with the slain dragon at his feet, and Hans Memling's 15th-century portrait of a young man. Lorenzo Lorto's masterpiece here is a melancholy portrait of a young man.

Paolo Veronese's *The Banquet in the House of Levi* dominates another room. Originally it was a *Last Supper*, commissioned for the dining hall of a monastery. With its elegant people, wandering dogs, and atmosphere of luxury and pleasure, the painting posed a problem for some ecclesiastical authorities. The local Inquisitor particularly disliked the dwarf and the soldiers on the right, who, from the Inquisitor's point of view, were at least German and probably Prot-

---

A Note on Museum Hours

Visiting hours in Venice's museums are often subject to major variations. Many visitors who have budgeted only 2 or 3 days for Venice often express disappointment when, for some unknown reason, a major attraction closes abruptly. When you arrive, check with the tourist office for a list of the latest open hours.

estant heretics. Veronese got away with just changing the name, and whatever it's called, it's a splendid painting.

Four large paintings by Tintoretto, noted for their swirling action and powerful drama, depict scenes from the life of St. Mark. Titian's majestic *Pietà* was the artist's last painting, intended for his tomb in the church of the Frari. St. Jerome, who kneels by the dead Christ, bears the features of the 90-year-old artist.

Gentile Bellini's stunning portrait of St. Mark's Square (1496), back in the days when the houses glistened with gold in the sun, will give you a sense of how little Venice has changed. Two great paintings by Tiepolo, in his precise and vivacious style, the *Exaltation of the Cross* and *Transportation of the Holy House* were originally intended to grace ceilings, but here we can study them without craning our necks.

Also of note is the cycle of narrative paintings that Vittore Carpaccio did of St. Ursula for the Scuola of Santa Orsola. The most famous is no. 578, showing Ursula asleep on her elongated bed, with a dog nestled on the floor nearby, as the angels come for a visitation.

The 18th century is also represented. Look for Canaletto's *Porticato* and paintings by Francesco Guardi before bidding farewell to this galaxy of great Venetian art.

Museo Civico Correr (Correr Civic Museum). In the Procuratie Nuove, Piazza San Marco (enter under the arcades of Ala Napoleonica at the western end of the square). ☎ **041/5-22-56-25.** Admission (including admission to Ducal Palace) 14,000L ($8.10) adults, 8,000L ($4.65) students 14–28, 4,000L ($2.30) children 6–14; free children 5 and under. Nov–Mar daily 9am–5pm; Apr–Oct daily 9am–7pm. Vaporetto: San Marco.

This museum traces the development of Venetian painting from the 14th to the 16th century. On the second floor are the red-and-maroon robes once worn by the doges, plus some fabulous street lanterns and an illustrated copy of *Marco Polo in Tartaria.* You can see Cosmé Tura's *Pietà,* a miniature of renown from the genius in the Ferrara School. This is one of his more gruesome works, depicting a bony, gnarled Christ sprawled on the lap of the Madonna. Farther on, search out Schiavone's *Madonna and Child* (no. 545), our candidate for ugliest child ever depicted on canvas (no wonder his mother looks askance).

One of the most important rooms boasts three masterpieces: a *Pietà* by Antonello da Messina, a *Crucifixion* by Flemish Hugo van der Goes, and a *Madonna and Child* by Dieric Bouts, who depicted the baby suckling his mother in a sensual manner. The star attraction of the Correr is the Bellini salon, which includes works by founding father Jacopo and his son, Gentile. But the real master of the household was the other son, Giovanni, the major painter of the 15th-century Venetian school (look for his *Crucifixion* and compare it with his father's treatment of the same subject). A small but celebrated portrait of St. Anthony of Padua by Alvise Vivarini is here, plus works by Bartolomeo Montagna. An important work is Vittore Carpaccio's *Two Venetian Ladies*, though their true gender is a subject of much debate. In Venice they're popularly known as "The Courtesans." A lesser work, *St. Peter*, depicting the saint with the daggers in him, hangs in the same room.

Ca' d'Oro. Calle Cadolo, Cannareggio. ☎ **041/5-23-87-90.** Admission 4,000L ($2.30), ages 16 and under admitted free. Daily 9am–1:30pm. Closed Jan 1, May 1, and Dec 25. Vaporetto: Ca' d'Oro.

The only problem with the use of this building as an art museum is that the architecture and decor of the Ca' d'Oro is so opulent it competes with the works. It was built in the early 1400s, and its name translates as "House of Gold," though the gilding that once covered its facade eroded away long ago, leaving softly textured pink and white stone carved into lacy Gothic patterns. Historians compare its majesty to that of the Ducal Palace. The building was meticulously restored in the early 20th century by philanthropist Baron Franchetti, who attached it to a smaller nearby palazzo (Ca' Duodo), today part of the Ca' d'Oro complex. The interconnected buildings contain the baron's valuable private collection of paintings, sculpture, and furniture, all donated to the Italian government during World War I.

You enter into a stunning courtyard, 50 yards from the vaporetto stop. The courtyard has a multicolored patterned marble floor and is filled with statuary. Proceed upstairs to the lavishly appointed palazzo. One of the gallery's major paintings is Titian's voluptuous *Venus.* She coyly covers one breast, but what about the other?

In a special niche reserved for the masterpiece of the Franchetti collection is Andrea Mantegna's icy-cold *St. Sebastian,* the central figure of which is riddled with what must be a record number of arrows. You'll also find works by Carpaccio. If you walk onto the loggia, you'll have one of the grandest views of the Grand Canal, a panorama that even inspired Lord Byron when he could take his eyes off the ladies.

Ca' Rezzonico. Fondamenta Rezzonico, Dorsoduro. ☎ **041/2-41-01-00.** Admission 12,000L ($6.95) adults, 8,000L ($4.65) children 12–18, 4,000L ($2.30) children 11 and under. Sat–Thurs 10am–4pm. Vaporetto: Ca' Rezzonico.

This 17th- and 18th-century palace along the Grand Canal is where Robert Browning set up his bachelor headquarters and eventually died in 1889. Pope Clement XIII also stayed here. It's a virtual treasure house, known for its baroque paintings and furniture. First you enter the Grand Ballroom with its allegorical ceiling, then proceed through lavishly embellished rooms with Venetian chandeliers, brocaded walls, portraits of patricians, tapestries, gilded furnishings, and touches of chinoiserie. At the end of the first walk is the Throne Room, with its allegorical ceilings by Giovanni Battista Tiepolo.

On the first floor you can walk out onto a balcony for a view of the Grand Canal as the aristocratic tenants of the 18th century saw it. Another group of rooms follows, including the library. In these salons, look for a bizarre collection of paintings: One, for example, depicts half-clothed women beating up a defenseless naked man (one Amazon is about to stick a pitchfork into his neck, another to crown him with a violin). In the adjoining room, another woman is hammering a spike through a man's skull.

Upstairs is a survey of 18th-century Venetian art. As you enter the main room from downstairs, head for the first salon on your right (facing the canal), which contains the best works, paintings from the brush of Pietro Longhi. His most famous work, *The Lady and the Hairdresser,* is the first canvas to the right on the entrance wall. Others depict the life of the idle Venetian rich. On the rest of the floor are bedchambers, a chapel, and salons—some with badly damaged frescoes, including a romp of satyrs.

✪ **Collezione Peggy Guggenheim (Peggy Guggenheim Collection).** In the Palazzo Venier dei Leoni, Calle San Cristoforo, Dorsoduro 701. ☎ **041/5-20-62-88.** Admission 12,000L ($6.95) adults, 8,000L ($4.65) students and children 16 and under. Wed–Mon 11am–6pm. Vaporetto: Accademia.

This is one of the most comprehensive and brilliant modern-art collections in the Western world and reveals both the foresight and the critical judgment of its founder. The collection is housed in an unfinished palazzo, the former Venetian home of Peggy Guggenheim, who died in 1979. In the tradition of her family, Peggy Guggenheim was a lifelong patron of contemporary painters and sculptors. In the 1940s, she founded the Art of This Century Gallery in New York in the 1940s, one of the most avant-garde galleries for the works of contemporary artists. Critics were impressed not only by the high quality of the artists she sponsored but also by her methods of displaying them.

As her private collection increased, she decided to find a larger showcase and selected Venice, long a haven for artists. While the

Solomon R. Guggenheim Museum was going up in New York City according to Frank Lloyd Wright's specifications, she was creating her own gallery here. You can wander through and enjoy art in an informal and relaxed way. Max Ernst was one of Peggy Guggenheim's early favorites (she even married him), as was Jackson Pollock (she provided a farmhouse where he could develop his painting technique). Displayed here are works not only by Pollock and Ernst, but also by Picasso (see his 1911 cubist *The Poet*), Duchamp, Chagall, Mondrian, Brancusi, Delvaux, and Dalí, plus a garden of modern sculpture with works by Giacometti, some of which he struggled to complete while resisting the amorous intentions of Marlene Dietrich. Temporary modern-art shows may be presented during winter. Since Peggy Guggenheim's death, the collection has been administered by the Solomon R. Guggenheim Foundation, which also operates New York's Guggenheim Museum. In the new wing are a museum shop and a cafe, overlooking the sculpture garden.

Museo Storico Navale (Naval History Museum) and Arsenale. Campo San Biasio, Castello 2148. ☎ **041/5-20-02-76.** Admission 3,500L ($2.05). Mon–Sat 8:45am–1:30pm. Closed holidays. Vaporetto: Arsenale.

The **Naval History Museum** is filled with cannons, ships' models, and fragments of old vessels dating from the days when Venice was supreme in the Adriatic. The prize exhibit is a gilded model of the *Bucintoro,* the great ship of the doge that surely would've made Cleopatra's barge look like an oil tanker. In addition, you'll find models of historic and modern fighting ships, local fishing and rowing craft, and a collection of 24 Chinese junks, as well as a number of maritime *ex voto* from churches of Naples.

If you walk along the canal as it branches off from the museum, you'll arrive at the **Ships' Pavilion** (about 270 yards from the museum and before the wooden bridge), where historic vessels are displayed. Proceeding along the canal, you'll soon reach the **Arsenale,** Campo dell'Arsenale, guarded by stone lions, Neptune with a trident, and other assorted ferocities. You'll spot it readily enough because of its two towers flanking the canal. In its day, the Arsenale turned out galley after galley at speeds usually associated with wartime production.

4 Churches & Guild Houses

Much of the great art of Venice lies in its churches and *scuole* (guild houses or fraternities). Most of the guild members were drawn from the rising bourgeoisie. The guilds were said to fulfill both the material and the spiritual needs of their (male) members, who often engaged in charitable works in honor of the saint for whom their scuola was named. Many of Venice's greatest artists, including Tintoretto, were commissioned to decorate these guild houses. Some created masterpieces you can still see today. Narrative canvases that depicted the lives of the saints were called *teleri*.

✪ **Scuola di San Rocco.** Campo San Rocco, San Polo 3058. ☎ 041/5-23-48-64. Admission 8,000L ($4.65) adults, 6,000L ($3.50) students under 26, 3,000L ($1.75) children. Mar 28–Nov 2 daily 9am–5:30pm; Nov 3–Mar 27 Mon–Fri 10am–1pm, Sat–Sun 10am–4pm. Closed Easter and Dec 25–Jan 1. Vaporetto: San Tomà; then walk straight onto Ramo Mondoler, which becomes Larga Prima; then take Salizzada San Rocco, which opens into Campo San Rocco.

Of all Venice's scuole, none is as richly embellished as this, filled with epic canvases by Tintoretto. The paintings sweep across the upper and lower halls, mesmerizing you with a kind of passion play. In the grand hall they depict New Testament scenes, devoted largely to episodes in the life of Mary (the *Flight into Egypt* is among the best). In the top gallery are works illustrating scenes from the Old and New Testaments, the most renowned being those devoted to the life of Christ. In a separate room is Tintoretto's masterpiece: his mammoth *Crucifixion*. In it he showed his dramatic scope and sense of grandeur as an artist, creating a deeply felt scene that fills you with the horror of systematic execution, thus transcending its original subject matter.

✪ **Scuola di San Giorgio degli Schiavoni.** Calle Furiani, Castello 3253A. ☎ 041/5-22-88-28. Admission 5,000L ($2.90). Tues–Sat 10am–12:30pm and 3–6pm, Sun 10am–12:30pm. Vaporetto: San Zaccaria.

At the St. Antonino Bridge (Fondamenta dei Furlani) is the second important guild house to visit. Between 1502 and 1509, Vittore Carpaccio painted a pictorial cycle here of exceptional merit and interest. Of enduring fame are his works of St. George and the dragon—these are our favorites in Venice and certainly the most delightful. For example, in one frame St. George charges the dragon on a field littered with half-eaten bodies and skulls. Gruesome? Not at all. Any moment you expect the director to call "Cut!" The pictures relating to St. Jerome are appealing but don't compete with St. George and his ferocious dragon.

Basilica di Santa Maria Gloriosa del Frari. Campo dei Frari, San Polo. ☎ 041/5-22-26-37. Admission 3,000L ($1.75); free after 3pm. Mon–Sat 9am–6pm, Sun 3–6pm. Vaporetto: San Tomà.

Known simply as the Frari, this Venetian Gothic church is only a short walk from the Scuola di San Rocco and is filled with some great art. The most famous work is Titian's *Assumption* over the main altar—a masterpiece of soaring beauty depicting the ascension of the Madonna on a cloud puffed up by floating cherubs. In her robe, but especially in the robe of one of the gaping saints below, "Titian red" dazzles as never before.

On the first altar to the right as you enter is Titian's second major work here—a *Madonna Enthroned,* painted for the Pesaro family in 1526. Although lacking the power and drama of the *Assumption,* it nevertheless is brilliant in its use of color and light effects. But Titian surely would turn redder than his Madonna's robes if he could see the latter-day neoclassical tomb built for him on the opposite wall. The kindest word for it: *large.*

Facing the tomb is a memorial to Canova, the Italian sculptor who led the revival of classicism. To return to more enduring art, head to the sacristy for a 1488 Giovanni Bellini triptych on wood; the Madonna is cool and serene, one of Bellini's finest portraits of the Virgin. Also see the almost primitive-looking wood carving by Donatello of St. John the Baptist.

Chiesa della Madonna dell'Orto. Campo dell'Orto, Cannaregio 3512. ☎ **041/71-99-33.** Admission 2,000L ($1.15). Mon–Sat 10am–5:30pm, Sun 3–5pm. Vaporetto: Madonna dell'Orto.

This church provides a good reason to walk to this fairly remote northern district. At the church on the lagoon you'll be paying your final respects to Tintoretto. The brick structure with a Gothic front is famed not only because of its paintings by that artist but also because the great master is buried in the chapel to the right of the main altar. At the high altar are his *Last Judgment* (on the right) and *Sacrifice of the Golden Calf* (left)—monumental paintings curving at the top like a Gothic arch. Over the doorway to the right of the altar is Tintoretto's superb portrayal of the presentation of Mary as a little girl at the temple. The composition is unusual in that Mary isn't the focal point; rather, a pointing woman bystander dominates the scene.

The first chapel to the right of the main altar contains a masterly work by Cima de Conegliano, showing the presentation of a sacrificial lamb to the saints (the plasticity of St. John's body evokes Michelangelo). In first chapel on the left, as you enter, notice the large photo of Giovanni Bellini's *Madonna and Child.* The original, which was especially noteworthy for its depiction of the eyes and mouths of the mother and child, was stolen as part of a well-publicized 1994 theft, and pending the possibility of its hoped-for return, the photograph was installed in its place. Two other pictures in the apse are *The Presentation of the Cross to St. Peter* and *The Beheading of St. Christopher.*

Chiesa di San Zaccaria. Campo San Zaccaria, Castello. ☎ **041/5-22-12-57.** Admission 2,000L ($1.15). Mon–Sat 10am–noon; daily 4–6pm. Vaporetto: San Zaccaria.

Behind St. Mark's Basilica is this Gothic church with a Renaissance facade. It's filled with works of art, notably Giovanni Bellini's restored *Madonna Enthroned,* painted with saints (second altar to the left). Many have found this to be one of Bellini's finest Madonnas, and it does have beautifully subdued coloring, though it appears rather static. Many worthwhile works lie in the main body of the church, but for a view of even more of them, apply to the sacristan for entrance to the church's museum, housed in an area once reserved exclusively for nuns. Here you'll find works by Tintoretto, Titian, Il Vecchio, Anthony van Dyck, and Bassano. The paintings aren't labeled, but the sacristan will point out the names of the artists. In the Sisters' Choir are five armchairs in which the Venetian doges of yore sat. And if you save the best for last, you can see the faded frescoes of Andrea del Castagno in the shrine honoring San Tarasio.

Basilica di San Giorgio Maggiore. San Giorgio Maggiore (across from Piazzetta San Marco). ☎ **041/5-22-78-27.** Basilica free; belfry elevator 3,000L ($1.75). Apr–Oct daily 9:30am–12:30pm and 2:30–6pm; Nov–Mar daily 10am–12:30pm and 2:30–4:30pm. Vaporetto: 82 (the Giudecca-bound vaporetto) from Riva degli Schiavoni; get off at the first stop, right in the church courtyard.

This church sits on the little island of San Giorgio Maggiore. The building was designed by Palladio, the great Renaissance architect—perhaps as a consolation prize since he wasn't chosen to rebuild the burned-out Doge's Palace. The logical rhythm of the Vicenza architect is played here on a grand scale. But inside it's almost too stark since Palladio wasn't much on gilded adornment. The chief art hangs on the main altar: two epic paintings by Tintoretto, the *Fall of Manna* to the left and the far more successful *Last Supper* to the right. It's interesting to compare Tintoretto's *Cena* with that of Veronese at the Accademia. Afterward you may want to take the elevator to the top of the belfry for a view of the greenery of the island itself, the lagoon, and the Doge's Palace across the way. It's unforgettable.

Santa Maria della Salute. Campo della Salute, Dorsoduro. ☎ **041/ 5-23-79-51.** Free admission, but offering expected; sacristy 2,000L ($1.15). Mar–Nov daily 9am–noon and 3–6pm; Dec–Feb daily 9am–noon and 3–5pm. Vaporetto: Salute.

Like the proud landmark it is, La Salute—the pinnacle of the baroque movement in Venice—stands at the mouth of the Grand Canal overlooking Piazzetta San Marco and opening onto Campo della Salute. One of Venice's most historic churches, it was built by Longhena in the 17th century (work began in 1631) as an offering to the Virgin for delivering the city from the plague. Longhena, almost unknown when he got the commission, dedicated half a century to working on this church and died 5 years before the long-lasting job was completed. Surmounted by a great cupola, the octagonal basilica makes for an interesting visit, as it houses a small art gallery in its sacristy (tip the custodian), which includes a marriage feast of Cana by Tintoretto, allegorical paintings on the ceiling by Titian, a mounted St. Mark, and poor St. Sebastian with his inevitable arrow.

Santi Giovanni e Paolo Basilica. Campo SS. Giovanni e Paolo, Castello 6363. ☎ **041/5-23-59-13.** Free admission. Daily 7:30am–12:30pm and 3–7:15pm. Vaporetto: Rialto or Fondamenta Nuove.

This church, also known as Zanipolo, is called the unofficial pantheon of Venice since it houses the tombs of many doges. The great Gothic church was built during the 13th and 14th centuries. Inside it contains work by many of the most noted Venetian painters. As you enter (right aisle), you'll find a retable by Giovanni Bellini (which includes a St. Sebastian filled with arrows). In the Rosary Chapel are ceilings by Veronese depicting New Testament scenes, including *The Assumption of the Madonna.*

To the right of the church in the large campo is the **equestrian statue of Bartolomeo Colleoni,** the Renaissance condottiere who defended Venice's interests at the height of its power. It was sculpted in the 15th century by the Florentine Andrea del Verrochio. It is considered one of the world's greatest equestrian monuments, and Verrochio's masterpiece.

To the left of the pantheon is the **Scuola di San Marco,** with a stunning Renaissance facade (it's now run as a civic hospital). The church requests that Sunday visits be of a religious nature, rather than for aesthetic purposes.

5 The Ghetto

The Ghetto of Venice, called the ✪ **Ghetto Nuovo,** was instituted in 1516 by the Venetian Republic in the Cannaregio district, in the northwestern corner of the city. It's considered to be the first ghetto in the world and also the best kept. The word *geto* comes from the Venetian dialect and means "foundry." Originally there were two iron foundries here where metals were fused.

Venetian Jews were confined to a walled area that was locked at night, and obliged to wear distinctive clothing. However, they also had the right to permanent residence in the city and were protected by law from arbitrary violence against their persons or property, a guarantee unthinkable at the time in the rest of Europe. During the Renaissance, the Ghetto supported a lively intellectual life. The rabbi-scholar Leon de Modena (1571–1648) was known throughout Europe, and the poet Sarah Coppio Sullem (1592–1641) presided over a salon that served as a meeting place for Christian and Jewish scholars. Venice was one of the few safe havens in Western Europe for Jews fleeing from persecution during the Reformation and Counter-Reformation. Napoléon tore down the gates of the Ghetto, and the walls that once enclosed it disappeared long ago, but much remains of the past.

There are five synagogues in Venice, built during the 16th century, and each represents a radically different religious, aesthetic, and cultural point of view. The oldest is the **Scola Tedesca** (German synagogue), restored after the end of World War II with funds from Germany. Others are the **Spanish** (the oldest continuously functioning synagogue in Europe), the **Italian,** the **Levantine-Oriental** (also known as the Turkish Synagogue), and the **Scuola Canton.**

The best way to visit the synagogues is to take one of the guided tours departing from the **Museo Comunità Ebraica,** Campo di Ghetto Nuovo 2902B (☎ **041/715-359**). It contains a small but worthy collection of artifacts pertaining to the Jewish community of Venice but is by no means the focal point of your experience here: More worthwhile are the walking tours that begin and end at its premises. Tours last for 45 to 50 minutes each, incorporating a brisk commentary and stroll through the neighborhood and visits to the interior of three of the five synagogues. (The ones you visit depend on a series of factors like the scheduling of religious services, the availability of a rabbi, and the progress of renovations at the time of your visit.) Guided tours cost 12,000L ($7) adults and 9,000L ($5) students; children under 7 are free. They depart Sunday to Friday hourly between 10:30am and 3:30pm October to May and hourly between 10:30am and 5:30pm June to September. Participation in one of the tours includes free entrance to the museum.

If you want to visit just the museum (which is a lot less informative than participation in one of the tours), it will cost 5,000L ($2.90) adults and 3,000L ($1.75) students; children under 7 are free. The museum is open Sunday to Friday: June to September 10am to 7pm and October to May 10am to 4:30pm.

6 Especially for Kids

Unlike any other European city, Venice seems made for kids—providing you don't mind issuing a lot of warnings about avoiding the edge of every canal you see (and you'll see plenty). The most exciting activity for children is a **gondola ride.** Gondoliers are usually very patient with children, explaining (in Italian) the intricacies of their craft, though their actual demonstrations are more effective in getting the point across. Later in the day you can take your child to the **glass-manufacturing works** at **Murano** (see chapter 10, "Side Trips from Venice"), where the intricacies of the craft of blowing glass will be demonstrated.

The one museum that seems to fascinate children the most is the **Naval History Museum and Arsenale** (see "Museums & Galleries," earlier in this chapter), where the glorious remnants of Venice's maritime past are presented. Children will love the collection of scale-model ships.

To cap the day, you can purchase a bag of corn from a street vendor so your child can feed the fat pigeons in **Piazza San Marco.**

7 Organized Tours

Tours through the streets and canals of Venice are distinctly different from tours through other cities of Italy because of the absence of traffic. You can always wander at will through the labyrinth of streets, but many visitors opt for a guided tour to at least familiarize themselves with the geography of the city.

American Express, Salizzada San Moisè, San Marco 1471 (☎ 041/5-20-08-44), which operates from a historic building a few steps from St. Mark's Square, offers an array of guided city tours. It's open for tours and travel arrangements Monday to Friday 9am to

5:30pm and Saturday 9am to 12:30pm. Here are some of the most popular offerings:

Daily at 9:10am, a 2-hour guided tour of the city departs from the front of the American Express building, costing 40,000L ($23). Sights include St. Mark's Square, the basilica, the Doge's Palace, the prison, and in some cases a demonstration of the art of Venetian glassblowing.

Daily between 3 and 5pm, a 2-hour guided tour incorporates visits to the exteriors of several palaces along Campo San Benetto and other sights of the city. The tour eventually crosses the Grand Canal to visit Santa Maria dei Frari (which contains the *Assumption* by Titian). The tour continues by gondola down the canal and eventually ends at the Rialto Bridge. The afternoon tour is 45,000L ($26), and the combined price for both tours is just 75,000L ($44).

The "Evening Serenade Tour," 50,000L ($29) per person, allows a nocturnal view of Venice accompanied by the sound of singing musicians in gondolas. From May to October there are two daily departures, 7 and 8pm, leaving from Campo Santa Maria del Giglio. Five to six occupants fit in each gondola. The experience lasts 50 minutes.

A "Tour of the Islands of the Venetian Lagoon," 25,000L ($14.50), departs twice daily, 9:30am and 2:30pm, and lasts 3 hours. You'll pass (but not land at) the islands of San Giorgio and San Francesco del Deserto and eventually land at Burano, Murano, and Torcello for brief tours of their churches and landmarks. This trip departs from and returns to the pier at Riva degli Schiavoni.

If you'd like more personalized tours, contact the **Venice Travel Advisory Service,** 22 Riverside Dr., New York, NY 10023 (☎ and fax **212/873-1964,** or 041/523-2379 in Venice). Born in New York City, Samantha Durell is a professional photographer who has lived and worked in Venice as a private tour guide for more than 10 years. Some locals claim she knows Venice far better than they do. She conducts orientation sessions and private walking tours day or night. She also assists with advance planning services and is an expert in making wedding arrangements for those who want to get married in Venice. Her expertise also includes advice on how to find out-of-the-way trattorie. In addition, she has a wealth of details about shopping, sightseeing, art, history, dining, and entertainment. Private guided tours are individually tailored to your needs.

Morning and afternoon tours, for a maximum of four people, last at least 4 to 5 hours and are $225 for two people and $50 for each extra person.

7

Venice Strolls

You'll be spending a lot of your time walking in Venice—you may even get lost once or twice. The walking tours below will help by guiding you around some of the most significant sites in Piazz San Marco and its vicinity.

WALKING TOUR 1

Piazza San Marco & the Doge's Palace

by Thomas Worthen

Start   Basilica of San Marco.

Finish   Basilica of San Marco.

Time   About 3 hours or more.

Best Times   Mornings (9 or 9:30am).

Worst Times   Afternoons, when crowds gather.

This is the heart of Venice, and there's enough to keep you busy for a week. Here you'll find the Basilica of San Marco, which was the spiritual heart of Venice, and the Doge's Palace, which was its political center. These are two of the world's great cultural treasures. The other buildings that surround the piazza have much to offer as well.

Piazza San Marco may be the most beautiful plaza in the world. It has always been Venice's ceremonial gathering place. Napoléon pronounced it "the most elegant drawing room in Europe." It's a wonderful place to stroll, to window shop, to listen to the cafe orchestras, and to watch pigeons attack tourists. The one thing you won't find is a rock concert. After Pink Floyd performed here in 1989, the piazza was so thoroughly trashed that the authorities have said "Never again!"

In the height of the tourist season you may want to ignore our itinerary and just go to what's open and available, since there can be a line just to get into the:

1. **Basilica of San Marco.** It was built in 832 to house the relics of St. Mark, brought here from Alexandria in Egypt by two

Piazza San Marco Walking Tour

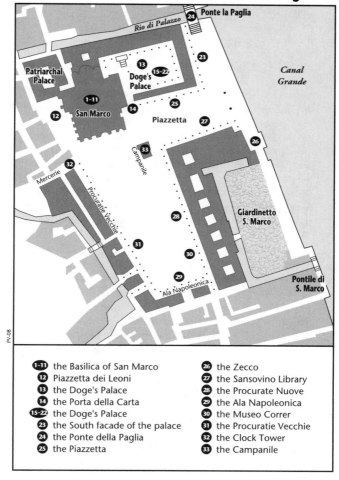

1-11 the Basilica of San Marco	**26** the Zecco
12 Piazzetta dei Leoni	**27** the Sansovino Library
13 the Doge's Palace	**28** the Procurate Nuove
14 the Porta della Carta	**29** the Ala Napoleonica
15-22 the Doge's Palace	**30** the Museo Correr
23 the South facade of the palace	**31** the Procuratie Vecchie
24 the Ponte della Paglia	**32** the Clock Tower
25 the Piazzetta	**33** the Campanile

Venetian merchants—or grave robbers, depending on your point of view. According to the legend, they took the holy man's body from its shrine in Alexandria with the help of some local Christians to prevent the precious relic from being desecrated by the Muslim rulers of Egypt. St. Mark himself was said to have made a few timely appearances to bless and abet the enterprise. The legend inspired many wonderful works of art, but it's at least as likely that the ruling doge at the time, Giustiniano Participazio, actually commissioned the theft to enhance his own prestige, and that of Venice. In any event, relics could not be owned but merely possessed, so *robbery* would certainly be too strong a word for this translocation of a spiritual treasure.

The Venetians based the design of their new church on that of the Church of the Apostles in Constantinople—then the richest city in Christendom—in order to announce architecturally that Venice was one of the great cities of the world with one of the really great relics. The church, built to honor St. Mark, has remained the most magnificent in Venice. The basic structure of the church you see today is mainly the result of a rebuilding that took place from around 1063 to 1094. The process of clothing the basilica in marble and mosaic was to take more than two additional centuries. The:

2. **principal facade** was originally plain brick. The columns, sculpture, and sheets of marble that cover it now are pure show. Since they're mainly spoils from elsewhere, they have a slightly hodge-podge quality, but because of careful attention to symmetry, the variety of colors and shapes is a delight. Venetian sculptors made free copies of some of the imported (or stolen) reliefs to maintain this symmetry. The large Byzantine relief of Hercules carrying a boar on the far left, just past the leftmost portal, is balanced by a Venetian carving of Hercules with a stag, on the far right. The Venetian imitation is less dignified and less classical, but it is also sharper, more energetic, and more decorative, like Venice itself.

Now stand just in front of the central doorway, and look up at the **three stone arches,** two below and one above the large mosaic of the Last Judgment. Here the sculptors were at their most original. The inner arch was created first and has the simplest figures carved in the lowest relief. As the sculptors proceeded to the second and third arches they became progressively more confident, and the relief of the carving becomes more pronounced, as well as more complex and naturalistic.

The outer faces of the upper two arches show such pious subjects as Virtues and Prophets. The insides of the arches—the parts you have to get underneath to see—are most interesting for the scenes they give us of 13th-century Venetian life. In the second arch, the inner face depicts the months, each illustrated with the

The Basilica of San Marco

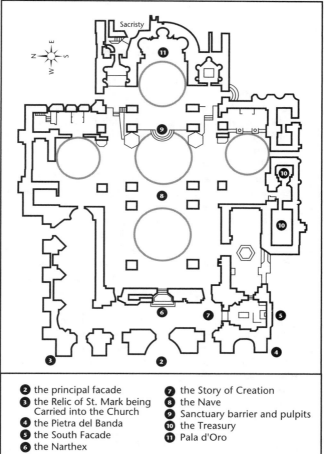

Sacristy

2 the principal facade
3 the Relic of St. Mark being Carried into the Church
4 the Pietra del Banda
5 the South Facade
6 the Narthex
7 the Story of Creation
8 the Nave
9 Sanctuary barrier and pulpits
10 the Treasury
11 Pala d'Oro

appropriate zodiac sign and a typical seasonal labor. The inside of the third arch, the one surrounding the mosaic, shows a number of specifically Venetian occupations, such as fishing (in the lower right) and shipbuilding (in the lower left), just above the seated man with crutches. According to tradition, that seated man was the architect of San Marco; however, he probably represents old age, when men can no longer practice their occupations.

Only around the year 1400 were the standing saints added to the very top of the facade.

Above the central portal, in front of the large window, are statues of four horses, the ***Triumphal Quadriga.*** These were the most spectacular of the trophies sent from Constantinople by Doge Enrico Dandolo, and when they were installed here they were the only freestanding works of sculpture on the facade. As one of Venice's greatest treasures, they became something of a symbol of the Republic's greatness. According to legend, the Four Horses of St. Mark's once stood at the hippodrome in Constantinople, and before that they decorated Nero's arch in Rome. Napoléon had them carted off to Paris after he seized Venice in 1797. In Paris they graced the Triumphal Arch of the Carousel for 18 years, but they were returned to Venice after the Battle of Waterloo. What you see today are actually copies, made in 1982. The originals are in the church's museum.

The four semicircular mosaics above the side doors illustrate the story of the theft of the body of St. Mark, while the four large mosaics on the second story depict the death and resurrection of Jesus Christ. Most of them were made in the 17th century as replacements for the original Byzantine-style mosaics, which were then totally out of fashion.

One 13th-century mosaic mercifully escaped destruction, the one above the doorway on the far left, which shows:

3. The relic of St. Mark being carried into the church. This lovely mosaic depicts San Marco as it was around 1260 when the mosaic was laid and when the topmost part of the facade was much simpler.

Go to the other end of the main facade, where you'll find the:

4. Pietra del Banda, a short red column, really no more than a platform, which was probably brought from Acre late in the period of the Crusades. Decrees were publicly announced by an official who stood upon it. It was severely battered in 1902 when the bell tower collapsed and a lot of the rubble slid onto it.

Now go around the corner to the side of the church facing the Doge's Palace and the lagoon to see:

5. The south facade, a showcase for some of the finest loot. The most distinctive piece is the dark-red porphyry relief carving with four grim men, at the corner adjacent to the palace (near no. 15, below). These four are the Tetrarchs, who ruled the Roman Empire around A.D. 300; they, too, were brought from

Constantinople. A Venetian legend accounts for their presence here in a more appealing way—these are four Muslims who were turned to stone as they tried to carry off the treasury of San Marco, the exterior of which they adorn.

About 15 feet from the south facade are two highly decorated squared shafts. It had always been thought that they were trophies taken from the Genoese at Acre, but recently it has been proved that they came from a 6th-century church in Constantinople, destroyed by the Crusaders.

Return to the main facade and enter the church through the main door. As you do so, admire the 6th-century bronze doors with the lion's heads. (No prizes for guessing where the doors came from.) Inside the doorway is the:

6. **Narthex,** the porch of the church. It's a different world—dimmer, more delicately adorned, and with a soft, uncanny glow of golden light coming from the mosaics in the vaults overhead. The low late-afternoon sun shining into the narthex can turn this effect into a glittering blaze. On either side of the entryway into the church are miniature columns framing mosaic niches. These mosaics, from around 1100, the oldest surviving in San Marco, present us with austere but colorful Byzantine saints.

The larger mosaic in the half-dome above the door shows *St. Mark in Ecstasy* (1545). Here is a very different, boldly Renaissance conception of a saint, three-dimensional and energetic. It was designed by Titian, who wisely left the time-consuming and demanding job of inserting little cubes of stone and glass in wet mortar to a professional mosaicist.

The mosaics in the vaults that cap the narthex to the right and left depict scenes from the Old Testament.

Now go to your right (as you entered the narthex), and stand beneath the dome. When you look up into the dome you will see the:

7. *Story of Creation,* according to the Book of Genesis. Each of the 6 days of creation is represented by the appropriate number of dainty little winged women. The reason for this odd bit of symbolism is made clear if, while standing beneath the dome, you face 45° to the right of the door leading back into the piazza and look up at the middle row of scenes in the dome. Here you'll see the Lord blessing the Sabbath Day and making her holy.

A number of threadlike red lines run through the mosaics (you can see them clearly in the scene closest to the door to the church). The red lines outline sections of the mosaic that, because of their ruinous condition, had to be filled in by restorers. You can see similarly outlined areas in many of the other older mosaics.

Now return to the part of the narthex just before the main entrance to the church. If you're up to climbing 44 steep steps, then, with the soft glow of the narthex mosaics fresh in your mind, enter the small door to the left of the central portal and climb up to the **museum** (admission fee), which contains ancient paintings, manuscripts, and fabrics that were used in the church services. The unfinished brick vaults in the smaller rooms will help you imagine what the entire building must have looked like before it was covered with mosaics. The museum is especially worthwhile for the views you'll have of the piazza and the interior of the church.

In the room to the right of the top of the stairs you can study fragments of 14th-century mosaics close-up. The faces are lined with small squares of reds, greens, and blues as intense as in a Matisse. When seen from across the room, the brilliant colors make the faces vivid, but blend together in such a way that they're hardly visible individually.

Continue still farther into the museum and you'll come to the originals of the *Triumphal Quadriga,* the four magnificent horses brought from Constantinople in 1204, that were once on the facade of the building. In ancient Rome they had been harnessed to a bronze chariot carrying a bronze Roman emperor holding the reins.

If the church is extremely crowded, you might begin your tour from the balcony; otherwise, descend the stairs, go through the main door, and enter the church proper. The first part of the church is the:

8. Nave. If you come in the dead of winter and are very lucky, you may have the entire place to yourself, but more likely you'll find yourself in a dense throng with rather too many guides. Don't abandon hope or the building. Find a place to sit (you may have to go well into the church before you find an empty bench), and take time to gaze about.

The church is cross-shaped, covered by five domes. Three of the domes march in succession from the main door to the high altar. Another dome is above each of the arms of the cross (the transepts). The lower part of the church is covered with stone that's flatter and simpler than that in the porch. The alabaster columns are all functional. The walls are covered with sheets of marble, so cut and arranged that their veining creates symmetrical patterns.

When you look up into the vaults and mosaics, you enter (at least visually) a realm where everything massive and sharp is avoided. Even the edges of the arches are softened by the golden mosaics. In these vaults the Venetian mosaicists created their greatest masterpieces, all surrounded by a golden aura that W. B. Yeats called "God's holy fire." Light is important mainly to illumine and reflect off the mosaics; therefore, the windows were placed at the very bottom of the domes to be as unobtrusive as possible. There's a large circular Gothic rose window in the south transept that seems very out of place in this Byzantine-style building; it was added to provide light for ducal ceremonies and for the display of relics.

The three major domes between the door and the altar depict three forms of interaction between God and humanity. In the large dome immediately above as you enter the church is the Descent of the Holy Spirit, in the form of a dove, on Jesus' disciples. The great dome in the center of the church shows the Ascension of Christ into heaven. In the dome above the sanctuary is still another image of Christ, this time with the prophets who foretold his coming.

The arches between the domes and some of the walls have scenes from the life of Christ. On the arch between the first and second domes are some of the most beautiful narrative scenes in San Marco, illustrating Christ's death and resurrection with Byzantine restraint. On the right is the Crucifixion. On the top are the holy women visiting the empty tomb on Easter morning. On the left, opposite the Crucifixion, is Christ's journey to hell to liberate the souls of the righteous of the Old Testament. This last scene was the usual way of illustrating Christ's resurrection in Byzantine art.

The lesser domes, arches, and walls depict various saints and stories connected with St. Mark.

Many of the original mosaics have been replaced in the last 500 years. Sometimes the mosaicist simply copied the composition that had been here before. The apse above the high altar is Renaissance in date (1506) but very Byzantine in style. More often an artist was commissioned to design a new composition of the same subject, and these changes were generally for the worse.

Move on now to the:

9. Sanctuary barrier and pulpits. The culmination of any church is its sanctuary, the place around the altar reserved for the priests and choir. The rest of the church, where the congregation stands, is focused on it. It's separated architecturally by being raised up and enclosed by a screen. The stone slabs that form the parapet of the screen have, however, been put on hinges so that they can be opened for services (the 20th-century congregation has a much better view of the sanctuary than did earlier congregations).

Beneath the sanctuary is a many-columned crypt designed to contain the shrine of St. Mark. It's well below water level and was generally flooded until an impressive job of sealing, completed in 1993, rendered it dry for the first time in centuries. The crypt is accessible only for prayer.

On top of the screen, in the center, is a silver crucifix flanked by statues of Mary and John the Evangelist, and flanking this group are the 12 Apostles. These handsome Gothic figures, installed in 1396, may seem as inappropriate as the rose window, since there are usually no freestanding statues in a Byzantine-style church.

Immediately in front of the screen on either side is a pulpit. The one on the left, the green stone wedding cake topped with a bulging parapet and a canopy, was for reading the Bible. The reddish pulpit on the right was for the presentation of the doge to the people and the display of holy relics. In the 18th century, when the choir of San Marco was world famous, musicians would crowd into it to play for services.

Walk into the transept, beneath the dome, and turn right between the columns. In front of you is the:

10. Treasury (admission fee), which has the world's best collection of Byzantine treasures, together with a number of masterpieces made in Venice itself.

The very best treasure, however, is in the sanctuary, and requires still another admission fee. As you leave the treasury, move toward your right in the direction of the sanctuary, following the signs that say PALA D'ORO. The turnstile just beyond the ticket seller is more or less where the doge's throne would have been placed when the doge attended the service. After you pay, go around to the back of the high altar to see the:

11. Pala d'Oro (Golden Altarpiece), a stunning conglomeration of Byzantine enameling, gold, and jewels. According to a 1796 inventory, its decorations include 1,300 pearls, 400 garnets, 300 sapphires, 300 emeralds, 90 amethysts, 75 balases, 15 rubies, 4 topazes, and 2 cameos. Begun around 1105, it reached its present appearance only in 1342, enlarged and enriched through several centuries. It was made to face into the nave, and still does on the major feasts. Generally, however, it's turned in the opposite direction so that you can't look for free.

While you're in the sanctuary, admire the four richly carved alabaster columns that support the stone canopy above the altar. The figures in the arches illustrate the life of Christ. Scholars have argued about whether the columns were made in Constantinople in the 6th century or Venice in the 13th. The latter date is probably correct, but it hardly matters. Like so much else in San Marco, they're unique.

You'll probably leave the church on the side opposite the Doge's Palace, which will bring you to the:

12. Piazzetta dei Leoni (Small Square of the Lions), named for the two battered red Verona stone beasts (1722) that guard the well. Facing it, beneath the large arch (to your right if you left the church through the side door), is the noble tomb of Venice's 19th-century hero, Daniele Manin, who led the short-lived revival of the Venetian Republic from 1848 to 1849.

Now it's time to circle back to the other chief treasure of Venice, the:

13. Doge's Palace. It was begun in or shortly after 811 as a castle for the first duke, Agnolo Participazio. The palace has undergone several rebuildings and expansions, so no traces of the original structure are visible. The gracious Gothic structure we see today was not begun until around 1340 and was constructed in various stages over the next 100 years.

This palace remained the home of the doges (dukes) for almost a millennium, until the fall of the Venetian Republic in 1797; but the doge's actual living quarters were effectively reduced to four rooms. The purpose of the 14th-century rebuilding was to accommodate the various councils, offices, courts, prisons, and armories that were needed to make the palace not merely the town hall of the city of Venice but capital of the Venetian Empire as well. Unlike other medieval Italian governmental buildings, it's not a fortress. Its open loggias, picturesque decorations, and graceful structure bear witness to the security that the Venetian rulers felt here in the center of their stable, prosperous state.

There is sculpture at each corner of the building. On the level of the upper loggia is a protecting archangel. On the lower level are symbolic biblical scenes: *The Judgment of Solomon* is nearest the basilica, and *Adam and Eve* is at the opposite end of the facade near the piazzetta. There are delicate bits of symbolic sculpture on the capitals. Look for the ninth arch from the left on the upper loggia. Between these columns of red stone, death sentences were read.

The principal entrance to the palace is between the palace and the basilica, the:

14. Porta della Carta (Paper Door, perhaps named from the professional scribes who set up shop near here). It was built under Doge Francesco Foscari (in office 1423–57). Doge Foscari liked glory. He began the series of conquests of the mainland of Venice—conquests that ultimately turned Venice from an aggressive city of merchant gentlemen in the 14th century into a conservative city dominated by a landed aristocracy in the 18th. Foscari built this impressive and elaborate late-Gothic entrance to the Doge's Palace, with a statue of himself kneeling before a winged lion, the symbol of St. Mark and of Venice itself.

Napoléon liked glory too. After he conquered Venice in 1797, the French paid the chief stonemason, one Giacomo Gallini, 982 ducats to destroy all the lions of St. Mark in Venice. Though Giacomo took the money, this was one of the few lions his masons got around to chiseling off. It seems appropriate that the effigy of the man who began Venice's mainland empire should have been effaced by order of the man who destroyed it. The lion and the statue of the doge that you see today are 19th-century replacements.

Go through the entrance to the enormous stairway you see before you, the:

15. Scala dei Giganti (Stairway of the Giants). The stairway and the facade of the courtyard on that side were constructed after a fire gutted the east wing of the palace in 1483, to designs by Antonio Rizzo. The project was finished in 1501, but Rizzo didn't get to see it through—he had to flee Venice in 1489 when his overseers suspected that he was keeping about 15% of the construction funds for himself. The carved decoration here is derived from ancient Rome, but it's as delicate and charming—and as expensive and overdone—as the late-Gothic entryway that leads to it.

The Doge's Palace

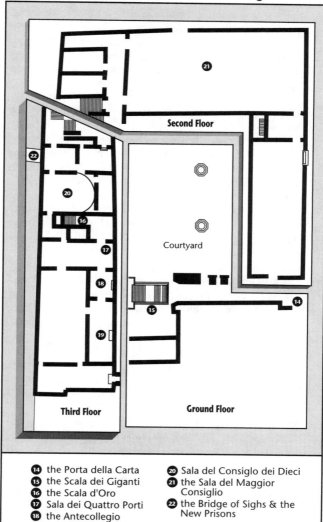

Second Floor

Courtyard

Third Floor

Ground Floor

⓮ the Porta della Carta
⓯ the Scala dei Giganti
⓰ the Scala d'Oro
⓱ Sala dei Quattro Porti
⓲ the Antecollegio
⓳ the Sala del Collegio

⓴ Sala del Consiglio dei Dieci
㉑ the Sala del Maggior Consiglio
㉒ the Bridge of Sighs & the New Prisons

The magnificent stairway takes its name from the two oversized statues of Neptune and Mars, carved by Jacopo Sansovino in 1554, that symbolize Venice's domination of the sea and the land. The stairway was principally a stage for such ceremonies as the coronation of the doge and the reception of important foreign dignitaries. Curiously, there's a jail cell beneath the stairs.

To go any farther you'll need to pay, but it's well worth it—the council rooms are decorated with some of the best art that Venice produced.

Your tour through the Palazzo Ducale will have to follow the path laid out for you. The following are some of the highlights and are (probably) in the order that you'll encounter them. But be warned that the mandatory path occasionally changes.

You'll first encounter the:

16. **Scala d'Oro** (Golden Stairs), the white-and-gold stairway that rises from the second floor. It was designed by Jacopo Sansovino (1554–58) to give important dignitaries a splendid access to the major reception and council rooms.

At the top of the stairs, turn right, and you'll be in the:

17. **Sala dei Quattro Porti** (Room of the Four Doors), really a staging area for three of the most important meeting rooms. The best thing in it is the painting on the long wall immediately to your right as you enter, *Doge Antonio Grimani Kneeling before Faith,* begun by Titian around 1555.

The next room on the itinerary is the:

18. **Antecollegio,** which has the loveliest collection of paintings in the palace. On the walls before you and behind you as you enter the room are four allegories (1577) by Tintoretto, filled with spiraling figures that are at once austere and sensuous. Each allegory combines pagan gods (symbolic of properties particularly propitious for Venice) with the four seasons to suggest that Venice is favored under all seasons and circumstances. If you face the door you came through, you'll see on your left, in winter, Vulcan, god of craftsmen. On your right are the three Graces in spring. Facing the opposite direction on your right is Ceres, goddess of prosperity, harvest, and summertime, separated by Wisdom (Minerva) from the harms of War (Mars). On your left, Bacchus, god of wine and of autumn, is married to Ariadne, even as Venice was wed to the sea.

On the wall opposite the windows, on your right, is Jacopo Bassano's *Return of Jacob into Canaan.* To the left of it is

Veronese's stunningly elegant and beautiful *Rape of Europa* (1580). We see the Phoenician princess, Europa, climbing in all innocence on the back of a white bull, who is Jupiter in disguise. Then, in several more distant scenes, we see him carrying her to the shore and across the Mediterranean, toward Crete, one of Venice's major possessions.

Next comes the:

19. **Sala del Collegio.** With its richly decorated ceiling and walls, it may well be the single most beautiful room in the palace. On the walls are glorifications of the virtues and piety of various 16th-century doges. Though there's a certain redundancy of Virgins and Christs, each work separately is quite handsome. As you enter, all the paintings to your right and behind you are by Tintoretto. The painting facing you is by Veronese, celebrating Doge Sebastian Falier and the Battle of Leponto (1581–82). Veronese also painted the allegorical scenes in the ceiling (1575–78); the large painting above the raised tribune is *Venice Enthroned, Honored by Justice and Peace.* The smaller figures in the ceiling represent the virtues of Venice. The woman knitting a spider web on your right, in the second ceiling panel from the entrance wall, for instance, is *Dialectic,* weaving (allegorically) a web of words.

The next room is a larger hall for the senate. The paintings (1585–95) are more extensive, if not necessarily of higher quality.

The exit returns you to the Room of the Four Doors. The painting on the easel is *Venice Honored by Neptune* (1745–50), by Tiepolo, one of the more recent paintings in the palace; the version above the windows is a copy. Next follows the:

20. **Sala del Consiglio dei Dieci** (Room of the Council of Ten), the meeting place of the most powerful committee in Venice. This council actually consisted of 17 people: the Council of Ten itself, the doge, and the doge's six counselors. The room's ceiling would be even more spectacular if the central painting hadn't been carted off to Paris during the Napoleonic occupation and replaced by a copy.

After this room, the tour can vary. You'll probably pass through the armory, and you may see fragments of some of the older works of art in the building, if that section is open. The two following sites are among the most memorable parts of the palace, though you may or may not see them in this order. The:

21. **Sala del Maggior Consiglio** (Room of the Great Council) was originally constructed between 1340 and 1355, but after being

gutted by fire in 1577, it was completely rebuilt. It needed to be big, since it had to seat every enfranchised citizen of Venice—all noblemen over the age of 25. Their average number was around 1,500, and their major function was to elect the officials in the other councils. There were nine double rows of seats, arranged back-to-back and running lengthwise down the hall. (The specific arrangement of seats can be seen in a display at the far end of the room.)

The ensemble of the decoration may be more spectacular than its parts, but two of the paintings are wonderful. The enormous scene on the end wall is *Paradise* (1588–94), by Tintoretto, one of the largest paintings on canvas in the world. The oval painting on the ceiling above it is the *Apotheosis of Venice,* by Paolo Veronese, the perfect embodiment of Venice's self-conception—elegant, wealthy, aristocratic, and most serene.

On the walls immediately beneath the ceiling are portraits of the doges. The most famous is the one who isn't here. Opposite *Paradise,* on the left, one of the portraits seems to be covered with a veil, and a text reads: "Here is the place of Marin Falier, beheaded for his crimes." In 1355, after a year in office, Doge Marin Falier attempted to overthrow the Republic in an effort to replace his ceremonial power with real power, but he underestimated the efficiency of the Venetian bureaucrats.

After passing through small barren corridors, you'll come to the:

22. Bridge of Sighs and the New Prisons (1566–1614). The bridge served as the link between the court and torture rooms in the Doge's Palace and the prisons on the other side of a small canal. The name "Bridge of Sighs" was a 19th-century romantic invention, but it's certainly appropriate and evocative.

The prisons continued to be used until 1919. The most famous prisoner here was Daniel Manin, the Venetian patriot, who was imprisoned here by the Austrians and later released in the 1848 rebellion. The famous and daring escape of another prisoner, Casanova, was made from an older prison, under the roof of the palace.

Much has been written about the evils of the Venetian judicial system, its use of secret denunciations and trials, political imprisonment, and torture. The piazzetta in front of the Doge's Palace was the traditional spot for state executions, and even in the Republic's eminently civilized later centuries these spectacles were gruesome. In 1595, Fynes Moryson, an Elizabethan traveler, witnessed the execution of two young men who were the sons of senators. Their hands were cut off and their tongues ripped from their throats before they were beheaded. Their crime had been a night of public drunkenness and wild behavior—their sentence may have had more to do with their failure to uphold standards expected of patricians than with their actual crime. William Lithgow, a Scottish visitor to Venice in 1610, reported seeing a friar "burning quick [that is, alive] at St. Mark's pillars for begetting 15 young noble nuns with child, and all within one year."

Still, similar methods were standard for the period, and the rulers of Venice instinctively avoided fanaticism. For its time Venice had one of the more equitable judicial systems. In the 18th century the Republic became the second country in the world to outlaw judicial torture.

At the end of your tour of the palace, you'll find yourself in the large courtyard. Note the two fantastically elaborate well heads (1556 and 1559), made of expensive bronze, not cheap stone.

After you leave the palace, you'll be beside the:

23. South facade of the palace. This was built before the facade near the basilica, and the sculptural details are even better. Each capital is elaborately carved, and each is different.

The bridge next to this corner is the:

24. Ponte del Paglia (Bridge of Straw). It was named not for the building material but for the cargo that was brought here. It offers a fine view of the Bridge of Sighs. Drowned bodies used to be placed nearby for relatives to claim, or, if unclaimed, to be buried by a charitable institution.

The sculpture at this corner of the Doge's Palace is the *Drunkenness of Noah,* whose three sons are just around the corner. Since those sons were supposed to have been the ancestors of all the races on the earth, this scene may suggest the breadth of Venetian trading enterprises.

Now go to the opposite end of the palace, to the two enormous columns, and you'll be in:

25. Piazzetta San Marco, the sea entrance to San Marco and the palace, with the two columns forming its gateway. This was the site of a variety of ceremonies and celebrations. From here the doge entered his ceremonial boat, *Bucentoro,* for his annual Marriage with the Sea ceremony on Ascension Day. During Carnevale, acrobats used to form huge human pyramids and some daredevil would slide down a rope to the piazzetta from the top of the campanile.

The enormous monolithic columns were trophies brought from the eastern Mediterranean in the 12th century and dedicated to Venice's patron saints. The one with the winged lion on the top is the Column of St. Mark. The lion was probably made around 300 B.C. in what is today southeastern Turkey, but the wings are Venetian additions. The other column supports St. Theodore, the pre-Mark patron saint of Venice; it's a hodge-podge of antique fragments standing on a Venetian dragon. Executions took place between the two columns, and to this day some Venetians are reluctant to walk between them.

The large building opposite the Doge's Palace is the library designed by Jacopo Sansovino, beginning in 1536, and called, appropriately, the Sansovino Library (see no. 27, below). It's a glorious building, "above envy," as Aretino said. Using nothing but white stone and shadows, Sansovino achieved an effect as rich and lush as that of its polychromed neighbors. No surprise that it was influential—and you'll see echoes of it along the Grand Canal.

If you go around the library, along the water and away from the Doge's Palace, the next building you'll come to is the:

26. **Zecco,** or mint. The shiny gold coins minted here were called *zecchini,* which gives us our word *sequin.* The facade of this knobby building is radically different from that of the library; strangely, the two were designed by the same man, Sansovino. The ponderous and rough stones suggest that the building is so strong that the gold within is safe. Originally it had only two stories, but because the furnaces made it intolerably hot, a third story was added in 1554 to help with ventilation.

The next part of the tour is a stroll alongside and through the porticoes that surround the Piazzetta and Piazza San Marco. Begin in the nearest one, the portico beneath the:

27. **Sansovino Library** (also called the Biblioteca Marciana, or Library of St. Mark). At no. 7 is the entrance to the library itself. Its greatest treasure is its collection of books printed in Venice; for until the end of the Republic, Venice was the most important book-printing center in Italy, at one time producing more books than the rest of the world combined. Its most famous press was that of Aldus Manutius, known especially for his beautiful and scrupulously correct editions of Greek and Latin classics.

No. 13A is the entrance to the **old library,** generally opened only for special exhibits. If the door is open, by all means go up, if only to see the richly decorated rooms with paintings by Veronese, Tintoretto, and Titian, among others. With a place this beautiful for study, it's surprising that Venice didn't produce more great writers.

No. 17 is the entrance to the **Museo Archeologico,** which has an excellent collection of sculpture from ancient Greece (remember that the Venetian Empire included many possessions in what is today Greece!) and Rome.

Shortly after, the portico takes a left-hand turn, then you'll be in the:

28. **Procuratie Nuove.** Built after 1586, it was conceived as a sort of extension of the Sansovino Library, with one floor too many. It served as the residence for the procurators, the most honored officials in Venice after the doge. Today it houses some of the city's more elegant shops and, on the upper floors, the Correr Museum (see no. 30, below).

No. 52 leads into a courtyard with the best collection of well heads in Venice and with an excellent explanatory text in English, just inside the door from the portico. If a doorkeeper should question your purpose, indicate that you want to see the *vere da pozzo* (well heads).

🕐 **TAKE A BREAK** A few doors down is the ✪ **Caffè Florian,** Piazza San Marco 56–59 (☎ **041/5-28-53-38**), a coffee shop that has been here since the middle of the 18th century. Casanova claimed to have stopped here for coffee after breaking out of his cell in the Doge's Palace, before fleeing Venice. From 1815 to 1866, during the years of the Austrian occupation, the Caffè Florian was a bastion of Venetian patriots. During the 1848–49 rebellion against Austria, the Florian for a time called itself the Manin, in honor of the leader of the insurrection. Later in the century, according to Ruskin, it was a place where "the idle Venetians of the middle classes lounge, and read empty journals." It's a real pleasure to sit at an outdoor table or in one of the hyperdecorated rooms (1858) and while away an hour conversing or reading an "empty journal," but it's a pleasure that doesn't come cheap.

Now turn into the portico that runs at a right angle to the one you've been in, the:

29. **Ala Napoleonica** (Napoleonic Wing), opposite the basilica. It was rebuilt under Napoléon (1808–14) to make a formal entrance

and a ballroom for the royal residence that he had constructed into the Procuratie Nuove. In the middle of this wing is a large passageway named for the Church of San Gimignano, torn down in 1808 for the greater glory of the French ruler. A representation of the facade of the church is set in the pavement in the middle of the passageway.

A grand, though chilly, neoclassical stairway rises from the passageway to the second floor and the:

30. **Museo Civico Correr,** which is really several connected museums. There are temporary exhibition galleries, with tickets sold at the foot of the stairs in the tourist season. This part is almost always worthwhile since the Correr hosts some of the finest temporary exhibitions in Venice. The first room of the exhibition hall is a magnificent neoclassical ballroom of 1822, designed by Lorenzo Santi, with pieces of sculpture by Venice's great neoclassical sculptor, Antonio Canova.

The main floor of the Correr Museum is dedicated to Venetian civilization, in both its more stately and its more intimate forms. Objects range from battle standards to *zoccoli,* the foot-high shoes that many upper-class women and prostitutes once tottered about in. Painted scenes range from ducal processions to battles between rival Venetian mobs at a parapetless bridge, with the losers cascading into the canal.

The museum continues on the next floor with the **Picture Gallery (Quadreria),** which features an excellent collection of earlier Venetian art, including what may be the earliest surviving Venetian panel painting (on a chest of around 1250). It's especially strong in paintings of the 14th and 15th centuries, and includes not only works by such Venetian artists as the Bellinis (Jacopo, Gentile, and Giovanni) and Carpaccio, but also some small masterpieces by their northern European contemporaries.

The last wing bordering the piazza is the:

31. **Procuratie Vecchie** (the older residence of the procurators), built between 1514 and 1526, again now with elegant shops on the ground floor.

Shortly after you turn into this wing you'll come upon two arches on your left that open into the **Bacino Orseolo,** which has probably the largest conglomeration of gondolas in the city (that is to say, in the world); and if you're interested in hiring one (and can afford it) this is a good staging point.

☕ **TAKE A BREAK** Continuing down the portico of the Procuratie Vecchie, you'll pass several cafes with their orchestras, including **Quadri,** Piazza San Marco 120–124 (☎ **041/ 5-22-21-05**), which the occupying Austrians patronized in the first half of the 19th century, while Venetian patriots were at Florian, across the piazza. Now the bands occasionally seem at loggerheads, but not the clientele.

At the end of the portico is the:

32. Torre dell'Orologio (Clock Tower), designed by Mauro Codussi and constructed between 1496 and 1499 with the two side wings added at a later time. It tells the time (to within 5 minutes), the phases of the moon, and the place of the sun in the zodiac. The clock is the city's most wondrous and beloved timepiece. At the top of the tower is a balustraded terrace from which two mechanical bronze statues, called "Moors" because of the dark color of the bronze, faithfully strike the hour on a massive bell. Just below, against a field of golden stars, a winged Lion of St. Mark looks out over the piazza and lagoon with his book open to the words "Peace unto you . . ." Below the lion, a niche contains a statue of the Madonna and Child. On Epiphany (January 6) and during the Feast of the Ascension, the clock's hourly pageant expands to include the Magi, led by an angel, who emerge from the doors on either side of the niche and bow before the figure of the Madonna. Legend has it that the eyes of the creators of the clock, Paolo and Carlo Rainieri, were put out to prevent them from ever matching this achievement for other patrons, but in actuality the two master clock makers received only solid praise and very solid pensions.

The arch beneath the tower marks the beginning of the Mercerie, the main shopping drag that connects San Marco and the Rialto.

Now that you've seen the piazza from the ground, you may want to see it from above. Return to the:

33. Campanile (Bell Tower). It collapsed on July 14, 1902, harming no one, apparently, but the watchman's cat. In the reconstruction, the original design (1511–14, by Bartolomeo Bon) was followed faithfully, but with a much more sophisticated understanding of building principles. It's unlikely to fall again soon.

At the base of the tower is a loggia that was begun in 1538 by Jacopo Sansovino, flattened in 1902, and carefully reconstructed by piecing together the original fragments as much as possible. It's a real jewel box and is decorated with some of Sansovino's finest statues. Originally it was a sort of clubhouse for nobles; now it's the entrance to the elevator going up the tower.

This is one of the two great tower views in Venice (the other is across the water at San Giorgio Maggiore). If the line here isn't too long, you can complete your tour of the piazza with a different perspective on what you've seen.

WALKING TOUR 2

The Accademia Bridge to Piazza San Marco

by Robert Ullian

Start   Accademia Bridge.

Finish   Piazza San Marco.

Time   Two or more hours, depending on the time you spend exploring museums or galleries.

Best Times   Weekday mornings or late afternoons, when the shops and galleries are open.

Worst Times   Midday or Sunday, when most places are closed.

Much of this walk will studiously avoid the parts of San Marco that visitors generally see anyway. Instead, it leads down side streets that take you into hidden neighborhoods and enclaves of interesting shop windows and galleries. The walk includes a visit to one church with a wonderful interior and a quick look at the exterior of another, but basically this is an odyssey of twisting explorations and small, unusual discoveries.

To start this tour, take vaporetto no. 1 to the Accademia stop and climb to the top of the:

1. **Accademia Bridge,** a wooden structure built in the 1930s (and redone in the 1980s) to replace the first Accademia Bridge, an iron span constructed by the Austrians in 1854. For both patriotic and aesthetic reasons, Venetians seem not to have fond memories of the original, which was demolished when traffic on the Grand Canal needed higher clearance. Most Venetians envision a permanent stone bridge here someday, but in recent years a proposal for a transparent plastic bridge that would not obstruct the vistas has gained some attention.

If you're coming from the Accademia side of the bridge, the view to the right is spectacular. Looking back toward the Dorsoduro side of the Grand Canal, the vista includes the white domes and towers of Longhena's baroque masterpiece, the Church of Santa Maria della Salute (completed in 1681). Ahead, on the invitingly gardened San Marco side of the Grand Canal, the first building to the right of the bridge is the 15th-century:

2. **Palazzo Franchetti,** adorned with lavish Gothic tracery and a large, beautifully tended canal-side garden created by the demolition of a *squero* (gondola building yard) in the 19th century. Heavily renovated in 1896 by the same Baron Franchetti who restored the Ca'd'Oro, the Palazzo Franchetti, though sumptuous, is not admired by purists.

The next two buildings to the right of the palazzo, separated from it by a narrow side canal, compose the:

3. **Palazzo Barbaro,** which was once the home of the family that glorified itself on the baroque facade of the nearby Church of Santa Maria Zobenigo. The older, closer part dates from 1425. The second part of the house, added in 1694, included a much-needed ballroom. The international glory of Palazzo Barbaro began in 1882, when the upper two floors were bought by Mr. and Mrs. Daniel Curtis of Boston, noted patrons of the arts: Robert Browning was invited to give recitations in the library. Henry James stayed while writing *The Aspern Papers;* he also used the palazzo as a setting for *The Wings of the Dove.* Claude Monet and John Singer Sargent each had a studio in the palazzo, and Whistler did a residence there. Cole Porter visited in 1923 before he moved to a floating nightclub moored outside the Salute.

From the left side of the Accademia Bridge, the first house on the San Marco side of the Grand Canal is the:

4. **Palazzo Marcello,** now the German Consulate, with a lush, overgrown garden to its side.

The large white palazzo immediately beyond is the:

5. **Palazzo Giustiniani-Lolin,** an early work by Longhena, completed in 1623 when the architect was in his early 20s. The sculptural baroque extravagances (like those on the Salute Church) that later became Longhena's hallmark are scarcely evident in this restrained, classic facade.

The next house to the left (if you stretch your neck to look and step back a bit toward the Dorsoduro side of the bridge) is the:

The Accademia to San Marco

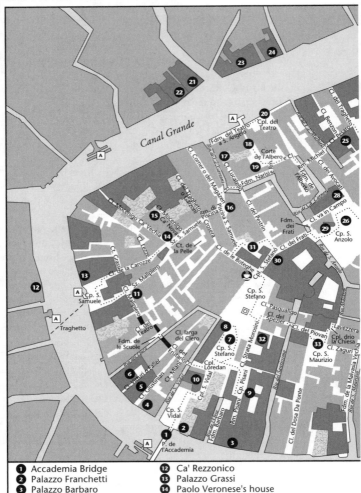

1. Accademia Bridge
2. Palazzo Franchetti
3. Palazzo Barbaro
4. Palazzo Marcello
5. Palazzo Giustiniani-Lolin
6. Palazzo Falier
7. Campo Santo Stefano
8. Palazzo Loredan
9. Palazzo Pisani
10. Church of San Vidal
11. Cassanova plaque
12. Ca' Rezzonico
13. Palazzo Grassi
14. Paolo Veronese's house
15. Calle Mocenigo Ca Nova
16. Piscina di San Samuele
17. Grand Canal palace land entrance
18. Corte dell'Albero
19. Nardi Houses
20. Campiello del Teatro and walkway
21. Palazzo Barbarigo della Terazza
22. Palazzo Pisani-Moretta

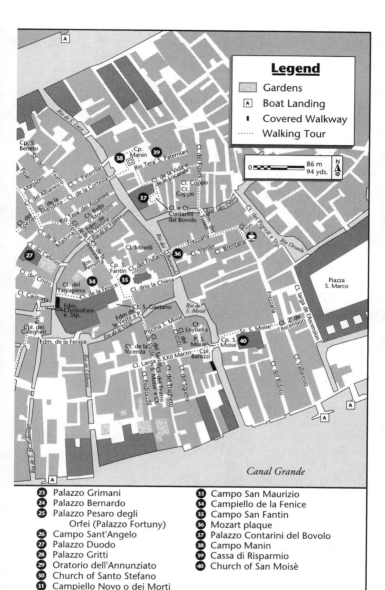

Legend

▨	Gardens
Ⓐ	Boat Landing
▮	Covered Walkway
⋯⋯	Walking Tour

0 ▭▭▭ 86 m
94 yds.

N

㉓	Palazzo Grimani
㉔	Palazzo Bernardo
㉕	Palazzo Pesaro degli
	Orfei (Palazzo Fortuny)
㉖	Campo Sant'Angelo
㉗	Palazzo Duodo
㉘	Palazzo Gritti
㉙	Oratorio dell'Annunziato
㉚	Church of Santo Stefano
㉛	Campiello Novo o dei Morti
㉜	Palazzo Morosini
㉝	Campo San Maurizio
㉞	Campiello de la Fenice
㉟	Campo San Fantin
㊱	Mozart plaque
㊲	Palazzo Contarini del Bovolo
㊳	Campo Manin
㊴	Cassa di Risparmio
㊵	Church of San Moisè

6. Palazzo Falier (early 15th century), with its two roofed terrace wings. Though they might seem to be a modern addition, they're really rare surviving examples of an old architectural form the Venetians called a *liago*. Such structures appear in Carpaccio's *Miracle of the Holy Cross* (in the Accademia), which depicts the busy area of the Rialto Bridge as it looked approximately 500 years ago. A branch of the Falier family produced Marin Falier, who, in 1355, became the only doge in the history of the Republic to be executed (he plotted to overthrow the Republic and seize power).

Directly ahead as you proceed across the bridge, you'll see the campanile of the Church of San Vidal, the parish church originally built in the 9th century by the Falier family, whose connection to this part of town is very ancient. Follow the way around to the right and then left, past the imposing pseudo-Palladian facade of the deconsecrated Church of San Vidal, and enter the spacious, sunny:

7. Campo Santo Stefano (also called Campo Francesco Morosini), the heart of the area this walk will explore. For now, we'll stay near the well head at the end of the *campo* (square) closest to the Accademia Bridge.

This fashionable campo, surrounded by a number of Venice's most unusual palazzi, was inhabited by some of the Republic's noblest families. It was also the address of some notable courtesans. For centuries, Venice's vast community of prostitutes was one of its main tourist attractions. In the late 16th century a directory for visitors was published, listing the names, addresses, and specialties of more than 11,000 such professionals (a copy can be seen at the Marciana Library). The campo was also the scene of bull-baiting spectacles; in 1802 the collapse of a grandstand here caused many injuries and led to the banning of this "sport" throughout Venice. A statue in the center of the campo commemorates Nicolo Tommaseo, who, along with Daniel Manin, led the insurrection against Austria in 1848–49.

From the well head, you are opposite the very long, low-slung Renaissance facade of the:

8. Palazzo Loredan. After the fall of the Republic in 1797, the palazzo was used to house a number of public institutions. Since 1892 it has been the home of the Veneto Institute of Science, Letters, and Arts. Check out the lavish Neptune door knocker on the main entrance, just beneath the central second-story row of eight balconied windows.

In the corner of the campo opposite the Palazzo Loredan is the immense:

9. Palazzo Pisani, which was begun in 1614 and continued to grow until the mid–18th century, at which time the Republic virtually put an end to further additions. With its formal, Romanesque-baroque style, this palazzo is unusual because its principal facade has always faced the campo rather than a canal, and because of its interior arcades, courtyards, and vast wings, which threatened to slowly encompass the entire neighborhood. Note the palazzo's own entrance campiello, sometimes used for outdoor performances, and the few small houses nearby that didn't get swallowed up as the palazzo grew. The palazzo now houses the Venice Conservatory of Music, as well as a banking house. Visitors are not generally welcome, but at times it's possible to see a bit of the interior during recitals, or, with luck, by sneaking in and asking about the school or concert programs when someone stops you.

From this side of the campo, look across to the:

10. Church of San Vidal (San Vitale), which now houses an art gallery. Notice how the monumental facade, an imitation of Palladio's San Giorgio Maggiore, seems misplaced against a building with so little depth. Inside, Carpaccio's *San Vitale and Other Saints* survives from earlier times.

☕ **TAKE A BREAK**   At the far end of the campo you'll see the austere wall of the side of the Church of Santo Stefano; to the left, across the calle from the entrance to the church, you'll find the **Gelateria Paolin,** Campo San Stefano, San Marco 2962A (☎ **041/5-22-55-76**), one of the best ice cream places in Venice, with flavors that are very rich and alive. You may not be in the mood to carry a cone or sherbet now, but we'll cross this campo a number of times, and, especially on a hot day, this is an option to keep in mind. Paolin is open Tuesday to Sunday from 7:30am to 8:30pm October to May and daily 7:30am to midnight June to September; closed December 15 to January 31.

We'll leave the palaces and facades behind for a while and enter another world via the narrow Calle de Frutariol, which starts between the side of the Church of San Vidal and the Palazzo Loredan. Follow this narrow passageway as it continues relatively straight though changing names, under a sotoportego and over a canal (check the view each way as you cross the small bridge). Just after the end of the second sotoportego, turn left onto Calle dei

Theatro, and then immediately onto the first right (Calle Malpiero), which goes under another sotoportego. It was on this street, once called Calle della Comedia, that Giovanni Giacomo Casanova (1725–98), the son of two actors in the nearby Theatro San Samuele, was born.

11. **A plaque at the end of the street,** just before the intersection with Salizzada Malpiero, conforms to the information in Casanova's autobiography, although no one can be certain in which house he was born or even if the events he recorded in his picaresque memoirs are in any way close to the truth. He became known as a libertine, spy, economist, philosopher, satirist, tax expert, and iconoclast, and we can only assume that Casanova's early years were spent planning how to escape to the glittering palaces and ballrooms only meters away from the world of his childhood.

At Salizzada Malpiero, look right at the flower boxes that adorn the buildings, but turn left, past the little-used Church of San Samuele, with its 12th-century campanile, and pass the vaporetto stop at Campo San Samuele, where you have a good view across the canal to:

12. **Ca' Rezzonico** (the large white palazzo to the right of the Ca' Rezzonico vaporetto stop). Designed by the baroque master Baldasare Longhena in 1657, though more reserved than Ca' Pesaro, his other landmark palazzo on the Grand Canal, Ca' Rezzonico was not completed until 1750—its top two floors were designed by Giorgio Massari. The Rezzonico family was legendary for its lavish entertainments; in 1758 they reached new heights of prestige when one of their members became Pope Clement XIII. He was the fifth Venetian to serve as pope.

In 1889 Robert Barrett Browning (known as "Pen"), the son of the poet Robert Browning, bought Ca' Rezzonico with the help of his wife, an American heiress, and together they refurbished the interior and built a chapel dedicated to Pen's mother, Elizabeth Barrett. They also installed a central heating system. Pen and his wife invited the 77-year-old Robert Browning, who had already spent much time in Venice, to join them in the palazzo, which the poet modestly described as "a quiet corner for my old age." Despite the heating system, Browning caught a chill and died there in December 1889. Ca' Rezzonico is now a museum of 18th-century Venetian art and furnishings (culled from many palaces) that gives you a sense of being in a still-functioning late baroque palazzo. The attic houses a puppet theater and a period pharmacy. (See chapter 6, "Exploring Venice," for details.)

In case you haven't already noticed the vast palazzo overpowering the far side of Campo San Samuele, you're facing Giorgio Massari's restrained, neoclassical:

13. Palazzo Grassi, built between 1748 and 1772. This was the last of the great houses to be constructed on the Grand Canal; the Grassi family, latecomers to Venetian high society, didn't buy their way into patrician status until 1718. After the fall of the Republic, the palazzo became a hotel for a time, and later a public bathhouse. In 1984 Fiat bought and refurbished the palazzo and converted it into a dazzling center for cultural and art exhibitions. The Palazzo Grassi's exhibits are beautifully mounted, often mobbed, and always worthwhile.

From Campo San Samuele, turn right onto Calle de le Carroze, and continue straight until it becomes the wider Salizada San Samuele, which contains a number of interesting shops and galleries, some good for a quick glance, others worth further inspection.

At no. 3338 is the comfortable but nonpalatial:

14. House of Paolo Veronese (1528–88), the last great painter of the Venetian Renaissance and a master of the use of illusion in decorative art. Among Veronese's early triumphs are the lighthearted trompe l'oeil wall paintings of Villa Barbaro at Maser that create optical illusions of servants coming through nonexistent doorways, children peering through elaborate windows, and beautiful women gazing down from balconies. Venice adored his magic and showered him with commissions. For a Dominican friars' refectory, Veronese painted *Last Supper* in the form of a lively and lavish Renaissance banqueting scene that some inside the church regarded as irreverent. Summoned before the Inquisition and ordered to change the painting, Veronese quickly complied by renaming the work *Banquet in the House of Levi.* Although (as his name indicates) Veronese was not a native Venetian, his work embodied the spirit of Venice at the height of its power—serenely joyful, poetic, and materially splendid.

Just past the house of Veronese, you might care to wander down the narrow:

15. Calle Mocenigo Ca' Nova. It doesn't look very interesting, but this was the land entrance to the Palazzo Mocenigo, a quadruple palace on the Grand Canal that was rented by British poet Lord

Byron in 1817, 2 years after the final defeat of Napoléon. The more spectacular entrances would have been made directly from the Grand Canal—and not merely by gondola. At times the romantic Byron would swim from the Lido up the Grand Canal to his house, with members of the foreign community perched at various locations en route to admire his sagging but still heroic spirit and figure. The comings and goings at the rear entrance were interesting as well. Byron's household consisted of a wolf, a fox, and a number of dogs, cats, birds, and monkeys; it also included a mistress who was the wife of a Venetian draper. Later an another mistress was added, called La Fornarina ("the little oven") because she was the wife of a baker. The fiery La Fornarina, whom he described as "energetic as a python," attacked Byron with a knife and then threw herself into the Grand Canal after being banished from the palazzo.

Another important British poet, Percy Bysshe Shelley, would also have trod this alleyway. He and his wife, Mary (author of *Frankenstein*), visited Byron in 1818, accompanied by Mary Shelley's stepsister, Claire Clairmont, who was Byron's former mistress. The 19-month-old Clara Allegra, Byron's daughter by Claire Clairmont, had already been in residence for some time, under the care of La Fornarina. There's much more (when Byron finally decamped from the palazzo, he did so in the company of a new 19-year-old mistress, Countess Teresa Guiccioli), but perhaps this will be enough to entice you to detour down this alleyway with its walled gardens and hidden mysteries. Byron completed several cantos of *Don Juan* while in Venice; he died in 1824 at the age of 36.

The next part of this walk will explore the beauty and eccentricity of this hidden part of San Marco. Continue straight up Salizada San Samuele, which narrows to become Ramo di Piscina, and ends at:

16. Piscina di San Samuele, a long, colorful courtyard. The name *piscina* indicates that this was once a pool or sleeve of water leading into a canal that has long since been filled in with earth. In earlier times a piscina would have been used for bathing, or for sheltering boats.

Walk to the left. At the end of Piscina San Samuele, the way diverges into three possibilities. Take the small stairway with the iron banisters on the extreme right. Follow the narrow bridgeway to the first cross passageway, and turn left into the Corte Lucatello, which is a worthwhile dead end leading to the:

17. **Land entrance** of one of the many elegantly renovated Grand Canal palaces. Now that private gondolas are history, this is the kind of daily route most palazzo dwellers must take, though not every palazzo is so pleasantly landscaped. Look through the gate into a secret garden, and beyond that, the *androne,* or water-level lobby. In this palazzo, you can see straight through the androne to the Grand Canal at the front of the building.

Retrace your steps, and walk a bit past the sotoportego on the left, then turn and look back. Roof gardens abound in this neighborhood—there's even one over the sotoportego. Go back and turn right under the sotoportego, which leads onto the canal-side Fondamenta Narisi. At the end you must turn left, and suddenly this traditional neighborhood has vanished. You're in:

18. **Corte dell'Albero.** Walk a bit to the left and you'll see what has swallowed up a good part of what used to be a neighborhood of narrow canals and calles, the massive:

19. **Nardi Houses,** built from 1909 to 1914. The Veneto-Byzantine and art nouveau touches on this rare example of a 20th-century Venetian apartment building help it blend into the architectural fabric of the city. The building is interesting, but it reminds us how fortunate it is that large parts of Venice were not demolished to create more such complexes.

As you face the Nardi Houses, turn right and follow the corte as it narrows and leads to the Grand Canal. Here you'll find:

20. **A tiny campiello** beside the Sant'Angelo vaporetto stop, and to the left, a rare walkway along the Grand Canal in front of the site where the **Tearto Sant'Angelo** once stood. We probably owe the existence of this small *fondamenta* (walkway) to the need for a landing spot to accommodate the many gondolas that once delivered the audience. This is the theater that produced many of Vivaldi's 40 operas.

Walk to your left, to the end of the fondamenta. The views from spots along the Grand Canal are always interesting. Directly across the Grand Canal, bordered by a rio, is the:

21. **Palazzo Barbarigo della Terrazza,** recognizable by its long side terrace with a white stone balustrade. Much of this palazzo's famed art collection eventually came into the possession of Czar Nicolas II. To the left of this palazzo is the large 15th-century:

22. **Palazzo Pisani-Moretta,** with its elaborate Gothic windows. This house still remains in the hands of the descendants of the Pisani family and retains much of its original furnishing and interior decoration.

If you walk to the far right end of the fondamenta, beside the vaporetto stop, and look across the canal to the right, you'll notice a white 3-story palazzo with triple arched windows in the center of its piani nobili. This is the:

23. Palazzo Grimani (1520), one of the first Renaissance houses in Venice. The second Gothic house to the right beyond that, with two Gothic water entrances and two floors of six Gothic central windows adorning its piani nobili, is the 15th-century:

24. Palazzo Bernardo, unusual because, if you look carefully, you can see that the two floors of central windows are out of line. Nonetheless, this is one of the most beautiful Gothic facades on the Grand Canal.

Retrace your steps to the Nardi Houses, turn left, and continue straight to the tiny short calle at the far end of the corte. When you reach the canal, turn right onto Fondamenta de l'Albero, then take a left on the first bridge you come to, which leads to Ramo Michiel. The way jogs slightly to the left as it crosses the next calle to become Calle Pesaro. As you come to the next short bridge, look to the right across the rio and you'll see the canal facade of the Palazzo Fortuny, the next stop on our walk. Continue straight along the side of the palazzo, then turn right into Campo San Benedetto, and at no. 3958 is the:

25. Palazzo Pesaro degli Orfei, or Palazzo Fortuny, bought at the end of the 19th century by the Spanish-born couturier, fabric designer, and photographer Mariano Fortuny y Madrazo (1871–1949). The palazzo now houses a museum of Fortuny's varied works and is also a venue for temporary exhibitions. At the turn of the century Fortuny invented and patented a method of pleating silk ("Fortuny-pleated" skirts are still produced today), from which he created diaphanous gowns popularized by Isadora Duncan, Eleanora Duse, Sarah Bernhardt, and other romantic heroines of that age. The wide-ranging private collection of Fortuny is interesting but uneven; the studio and living quarters of this versatile genius, as well as the unrestored Gothic palazzo with its courtyard, ancient staircase, and wooden loggia, are all fascinating. During popular exhibits, the number of people allowed to enter the building must be limited because of the palazzo's fragile structure. The Museo Fortuny is usually open Tuesday through Sunday from 9am to 7pm; closed Monday. Currently it is closed for restoration and is expected to open some time before the millennium; however, there may be delays so check its status with the tourist office before going there.

Exit the museum and enter Campo San Benedetto. From Campo San Benedetto, follow Calle a Fianco Ca' Pesaro to the right turn at the corner of the palazzo; at the sotoportego, turn left onto Rio Terrà de la Mandola until you reach the intersecting main thoroughfare, Calle de Spezier, where you turn right. You'll quickly enter the bright, open:

26. Campo Sant'Angelo. The first palazzo on the left side of the square is the:

27. Palazzo Duodo, and directly across, on the right side of the campo, is the:

28. Palazzo Gritti, unusual for its off-center doorway. Because they face onto dry land, these magnificent Gothic houses offer an unusual chance to study their carved stone ornamentation close-up.

To the right, in the center of the campo, is the tiny 12th-century:

29. Oratorio dell'Annunziato, which contains an *Annunciation* by Antonio Triva.

Walk straight across the campo, cross the Ponte dei Frati (enjoying views both ways), and continue straight. On your left, you'll come to the Gothic doorway of the:

30. Church of Santo Stefano, which was built in the 14th and 15th centuries. The interior of the church is filled with rich patterning—gold and pale silver paneled squares on the ship's-keel ceiling, peach and maroon brickwork design on the upper walls, floral frescoes on the arches dividing the naves, delicately carved and painted beam work crossing the central nave, and a garden of red and white marble columns leading to the Gothic tracery of the apse. The space is lit by high windows recessed into the sides of the roof. In the sacristy you'll find three late works by Tintoretto: *The Washing of the Feet, The Agony in the Garden,* and *The Last Supper;* behind the altar, you can see the elaborately carved 15th-century monks' choir. In the center of the nave is the tomb of Francesco Morosini, who was doge from 1688 to 1694. One of the Republic's great leaders, he reversed Venice's sagging fortunes by briefly reconquering the Peloponnese in Greece (see no. 32, below). The far door in the left aisle leads into the cloister, once covered with frescoes by Pordenone.

Exit the church, and turn left toward the campo. Just as you enter the campo, turn right onto Calle de le Boteghe, take the first right, and climb the steps into:

31. Campiello Novo o dei Morti (New Campiello or Campiello of the Dead). Today this spot is a pleasant discovery: a secluded plaza with gardens overhanging one wall and a terraced, vine-covered locanda (small hotel) at the right. The campiello's name, however, betrays a catastrophic history. The area was a mass grave for victims of the great plague of 1630, which accounts for its higher elevation. Until 1838 the site was closed to the public for health reasons.

Retrace your steps and enter Campo Santo Stefano. On the left side of the campo, just before it narrows, is the vast:

32. Palazzo Morosini, with its own courtyard in the corner of the campo. This was the family palace of Francesco Morosini (1619–94), who, during the Turkish invasion of Crete in 1669, held off 17 sorties and 32 assaults before finally surrendering his besieged garrison to overwhelmingly superior forces. Morosini returned to Venice and was relieved of his command, but he refused to accept defeat. Fifteen years later, sailing into battle with his beloved cat at his side (in the true spirit of Venetian eccentricity), Morosini led the Republic in the last successful military campaign of its history, the reconquest of the Peloponnese. Morosini is known to the rest of the world chiefly for lobbing a shell into the Parthenon, where the Turks were unfortunately storing gunpowder. Although the Parthenon had survived relatively intact until then, the explosion turned it into the ruin we know today. Morosini's bad luck with the Parthenon continued. Like Doge Enrico Dandolo, who had sent the *Triumphal Quadriga* back to Venice to adorn the Basilica of San Marco after the sack of Constantinople in 1204, Morosini envisioned sending home a spectacular trophy to mark his triumph. He chose the horses and chariot of the goddess Athena, which formed the western pediment of the Parthenon. In the attempt to dislodge the sculpture, however, it fell to the ground and was smashed beyond repair. Morosini was elected doge upon his return to Venice in 1688, and in 1694 he sailed off once more to fight the Turks. Again like Doge Enrico Dandolo, who had led a similar expedition in his old age 500 years earlier, Morosini died in the effort; within a few years, his conquests were recaptured by the Turks. Although Venice never made a cult of its leaders, this last hero of the Republic was gratefully revered. To commemorate Morosini's naval triumphs, a sculptured sea horse and various marine motifs adorn the main entrance of the palazzo. In 1894 the contents of the house were sold at auction. The embalmed body of his beloved cat is among the many Morosini possessions on display at the Museo Correr in Piazza San Marco.

One building to the left, as you face the Palazzo Morosini, is Calle dei Spezier, through which we'll exit the campo.

The shops on this street bespeak the neighborhood's elegance. As you cross the small bridge, look left and you'll see that the apse of the Church of Santo Stefano has been built over the canal and that only low canal traffic can pass beneath it. A few feet beyond, is the reserved, patrician:

33. Campo San Maurizio, with its neoclassical church, which was rebuilt from 1806 to 1828. We're in the antiques-gallery district of Venice, and this campo hosts occasional outdoor antiques markets; check with the Tourist Information Office if you're interested.

As you face the Church of San Maurizio, enter the narrow passageway to the right, which leads to a rabbit hole of twists and turns. Bear to the right, and take a right at Calle Lavezzera; at the sotoportego at the end of the calle, turn left onto Fondamenta de la Malvasia Vecchia, which ends at an angled bridge. Proceed straight into Campiello dei Caligari (the shoemakers' campiello), and exit through the ramp on the far right at the opposite side of the campiello. From this street, turn onto the first right, Fondamenta Cristoforo, which becomes a bridge. At the end of the bridge, a sotoportego takes you to the left. Turn right onto Calle de la Fenice. Turn left into the second corte you pass, the delightful, vine-trellised:

34. Campiello de la Fenice, with the Hotel La Fenice et des Artistces on its left side. At the left corner of the far end of the campiello, an interesting sequence of sotoportegos eventually leads back toward Campo Sant'Angelo. The building at the end of the campiello bears a plaque dedicated to the memory of those who died in the 1848–49 insurrection against Austria.

A right turn at the end of the campiello, and then the next right turn, will lead you to:

35. Campo San Fantin and, on your right, the remains of the legendary Fenice Theater, built in 1792 during the very last days of the Republic and destroyed by fire in January 1996. (Controversy over its rebuilding is still going on.) Venice was the first city to have public performances of opera, and the jewel-like 1,500-seat oval interior of the Fenice saw the world premieres of Verdi's *Rigoletto, La Traviata,* and *Simon Boccanegra,* as well as Stravinsky's *Rake's Progress* (in 1951) and Benjamin Britten's *Turn of the Screw.* During the years of the Austrian occupation (and especially during productions of works by Verdi) the Fenice was a rallying point for patriotic fervor.

The Church of San Fantin, opposite the site of the theater, contains a beautiful Renaissance dome by Sansovino over its apse. At the head of the campo is the Venetian Athenium, formerly the Scuola della Buona Morte, a confraternity that comforted prisoners condemned to death.

As you face the Church of San Fantin, exit the campo via the street to the left of the church, Calle dei Fruitariol, which is home to a number of the city's most stylish and personal shops and galleries. As you cross the bridge, look to the right across the rio at:

36. **The elegantly worded plaque** on the side of the building that declares that "the city of Vivaldi and Goldoni" wished to record that the young Salzburger, Wolfgang Amadeus Mozart, festively sojourned during the Carnevale of 1771.

Beyond the bridge, the name of the calle changes to Frezzeria (street of the arrow-makers).

☕ **TAKE A BREAK**   We're almost at the end of the walk, but if you'd like to stop for a fast, inexpensive meal, **Le Chat Qui Rit,** Calle Frezzeria 1131 (☎ **041/5-22-90-86**), a self-service cafeteria, is a good bet for soup or a quick bite. Follow Frezzaria until it makes a 90° turn; turn right and then immediately left. The restaurant is just on that corner. There are lots of rustic dining areas from which to choose, but they can be mobbed at mealtimes or when a tour group comes through.

To continue the tour, retrace your steps, and take a right onto the upmarket Ramo Fusieri. Continue over the bridge, along the narrowing but busy calle; opposite no. 4460, turn right onto Calle de la Vida o de Locanda (Street of Life or of the Small Inn); continue until you turn left onto Calle de Contarini dal Bovolo. On the left side of this narrow calle, you'll see the:

37. **Palazzo Contarini del Bovolo,** with its famous spiral-staircase tower and airy arcaded loggia, constructed in 1499. The large Contarini family built many palaces in Venice, each with its own identifying nickname—in this case, Bovolo comes from the Venetian word for "snail shell." Outdoor staircases were the rule in older palaces, but the Bovolo is unique. During the 19th century the palace changed hands a number of times and even served as a hotel for a time; it now houses an educational foundation. The ivy-covered garden has become a repository for architectural fragments and carved well heads and is home to many local cats. The canal facade of this palace is unremarkable.

Retrace your steps to the intersection with Calle de la Vida, but at that point turn left. Then take the first right turn, which will lead you into the bustling:

38. **Campo Manin,** named for Daniele Manin, leader of the 1848–49 insurrection against Austria (his house was on this plaza; looking from the statue of Manin, it's next to the left of the two bridges at the end of the campo). The opposite end of the campo is graced by one of the city's few prominently placed modern buildings, the:

39. **Main bank offices of the Cassa di Risparmio** (1964), designed by the noted architects Angelo Scattolin and Pier Luigi Nervi.

Exit Campo Manin by the left bridge as you face away from the statue of Manin. Continue straight on Calle de la Cortesia, a busy shopping street which changes its name to Calle de la Mandola. Make a right turn onto Calle de la Verona, which will lead you back to Campo San Fantin. Continue straight across the campo, exit on Calle del Cafetier, and keep straight until this sequence of calles ends at Calle Larga XXII Marzo, a broad pedestrian street built in the 1870s and named for the date of the establishment of Manin's new republic in 1848. Turn left onto this important shopping calle. The dominant feature of this street, of course, is the:

40. **Church of San Moisè,** originally founded in the 8th century. The current church building dates from 1632, with its facade designed by Alessandro Tremignon in 1668 and many sculptural decorations added by Heinrich Meyring in the 1680s to create a wildly rococo presence. You either love this extravaganza or hate it. Ruskin considered the facade "one of the basest examples of the basest school of the Renaissance." Inside, Meyring created an extraordinary sculptural altarpiece in the form of Moses receiving the Ten Commandments on Mount Sinai. Venice had an unusual tradition of naming some of its churches for Old Testament figures. Not quite like anything else in Venice, San Moisè might well be translated as "Holy Moses."

To the left of San Moisè is Salizada San Moisè, which will lead you back to Piazza San Marco and the end of this stroll.

8

Shopping

*V*enetian glass and Venetian lace are known throughout the world. However, there are so many shoddy imitations that selecting quality products of either craft requires a shrewd eye. Some of the glassware hawked isn't worth the cost of shipping it home. Yet other pieces represent some of the world's finest artistic and ornamental glass. Murano is the island where glass is made, and the women of Burano put in painstaking hours turning out lace. If you're interested in some little glass souvenir, perhaps an animal or a bird, you'll find such items sold in shops all over Venice.

1 The Shopping Scene

All the main shopping streets, even the side streets, are touristy and overrun. The greatest concentration of shops is around Piazza San Marco and around the Rialto. Prices are much higher at San Marco, but the quality of merchandise is also higher.

There are two major **shopping strolls** in Venice. First, from Piazza San Marco you can stroll toward the spacious Campo Morosini. You just follow one shop-lined street all the way to its end (though the name changes several times along the way). You begin at Salizzada San Moisè, which becomes Via XXII Marzo and then Calle delle Ostreghe, before it opens onto Campo Santa Maria Zobenigo. The street then narrows again and changes its name to Calle Zaguri before widening once more into Campo San Maurizio, finally becoming Calle Piovan before it reaches Campo Morosini. The only deviation from this tour is a detour down Calle Vallaressa, lying between San Moisè and the Grand Canal, which is one of the major shopping arteries with some of the biggest designer names.

The other great stroll wanders from Piazza San Marco to the Rialto in a succession of streets collectively known as the **Mercerie.** It's virtually impossible to get lost because each street name is preceded by the word *merceria,* such as Merceria dell'Orologio, which begins near the clock tower in Piazza San Marco. Many commercial establishments—mainly shops—line the Mercerie before it reaches the Rialto, which then explodes into one vast shopping emporium.

TAX REFUNDS   As a member of the European Union, Italy imposes a **value-added tax (IVA)** on most goods and services sold within its borders. If you're a resident of any country that's not a member of the European Union and spend more than 300,000L ($174) at any one store (regardless of how many individual items are involved), you're entitled to a refund of the IVA.

At the time of your purchase, be sure to get a receipt and an official IVA refund form from the vendor. When you leave Italy, find an Italian Customs agent at the airport (or at the point of your exit from the country if you're traveling by train, bus, or car). The agent will want to see the item you've bought, confirm that it's physically leaving Italy, and then stamp the IVA refund form.

In some cases, including leaving Italy via one of the larger airports, you can receive a cash refund directly on the spot. If the point of departure you've selected doesn't offer this (many highway and border crossings don't), you should mail the stamped form (keeping a photocopy for your records) back to the address indicated on your IVA refund form. Sooner or later, you'll receive a refund of the tax you paid at the time of your purchase. Reputable stores view this as a matter of ordinary paperwork and are very businesslike about it. Less honorable stores might lose your dossier or be unwilling to provide the forms you'll need. It pays to deal with established vendors on purchases of this size. You can also request the refund be credited to the credit card with which you made the purchase.

SHOPPING HOURS   Most stores open at 9 or 10am, many closing for lunch around 1 or 1:30pm, reopening from 3 to 7:30pm. Many also close on Monday morning and reduce winter hours when business is bad.

2   Tips on Shopping for Glass & Lace

SHOPPING FOR GLASS   Venice is literally crammed with glass shops: It's estimated there are at least 1,000 in the San Marco sestiere alone. Unless you go to a top-quality reliable dealer, like those we recommend, you'll often find both shoddy and high-quality glassware for sale at the same shop. Only the trained eye can always tell the difference. The big secret (which is becoming less a secret all the time) is that much so-called Venetian glass isn't Venetian at all but from former Eastern Bloc countries, including the Czech Republic. (Of course, the Czech Republic has some of the finest glassmakers in Europe, so that may not be bad either.) It boils down to this: If you like an item, buy it. It may not be high quality, but then again,

high-quality glassware can cost thousands of dollars. If you're looking for an heirloom, stick to such award-winning houses as Pauly &
Co. and Venini. Even buyers of glassware for distribution outlets in
other parts of the world have been fooled by the vast array of glass
in Venice. If even a buyer can be tricked, the layperson has only his
or her own good instincts to follow.

SHOPPING FOR LACE   Most of the lace vendors are centered
around Piazza San Marco. Though high, the prices of Venetian lace
are still reasonable considering the painstaking work that goes into
it. A small handkerchief with a floral border can sell for as little as
5,000L ($2.90); however, for large items like an heirloom-quality
hand-worked tablecloth, the sky's the limit. Much of the lace is
shoddy, and some of it (a lot of it, really) isn't Venetian lace, but
machine made in who knows what country.

The name in Venetian lace is Jesurum, which has stood for quality
since the last century. It has its own lace makers and, to guarantee
its future, even has a school to teach apprentices how to make lace.
Jesurum offers the most expensive, but also the highest quality, lace
in Venice. At other places you take your chances. The lace shops are
like the glassware outlets. They sell the shoddy, the machine-made,
and the exquisite handmade pieces. Sometimes only the trained eye
can tell the difference. Again, the best advice is to buy what you like,
if you think the price is reasonable. However, even if a piece is handmade, you can never be sure exactly where it was handmade. Maybe
China.

3   Shopping A to Z

ANTIQUES

Antichita Santomanco. Calle Frezzeria, San Marco 1504. ☎ **041/
5-23-66-43.** Vaporetto: San Marco.

This store is for the specialist only—especially the well-heeled specialist. It deals in antique furniture, books, prints, and coins. Of
course, the merchandise is ever-changing, but you're likely to pick
up some little heirloom item in the midst of the clutter. Many of the
items date from the Venetian heyday of the 1600s.

BOOKSTORES

Libreria San Giorgio. Calle Larga XXII Marzo, San Marco 2087. ☎ **041/
5-23-84-51.** Vaporetto: San Marco.

Near the American Express office, this bookstore has several specialties, one of which is books on Venetian art, including Tiepolo.

Libreria Sansovino. Bacino Orseolo, San Marco 84. ☎ **041/5-22-26-23.**
Vaporetto: San Marco.

This store is centrally located to the north of Piazza San Marco. It carries both hard- and softcover books in English as well as books on art, literature, and history.

BRASS OBJECTS

○ **Valese Fonditore.** Calle Fiubera, San Marco 793. ☎ **041/5-22-72-82.**
Vaporetto: San Marco.

Founded in 1913, Valese Fonditore serves as a showcase for one of the most famous of the several foundries that make their headquarters in Venice. Many of the brass copies of 18th-century chandeliers produced by this company grace fine homes in the United States. Many visitors to Venice invest in these brass castings, which eventually become family heirlooms. If you're looking for a brass replica of the sea horses decorating the sides of gondolas, this shop stocks them in five or six styles and sizes. A pair of medium-sized ones, each about 11 inches tall, begins at 320,000L ($185.60).

DOLLS

Bambole di Frilly. Fondamenta dell'Osmarin, Castello 4974. ☎ **041/521-2579.** Vaporetto: Mto. Vittorio Emanuele.

This studio/shop offers dolls with meticulously painted porcelain faces (they call it a "biscuit") and hand-tailored costumes, including dressy pinafores. The reasonably priced smaller dolls are made with the same painstaking care, offering a real souvenir value. Prices begin at 28,000L ($16.25) and can go as high as 1,500,000L ($870).

FASHION

○ **Belvest Boutique.** Calle Vallaresso, San Marco 1305 (near Harry's Bar).
☎ **041/5-28-79-33.** Vaporetto: San Marco.

This is one of the finest boutiques, specializing in clothing for women and men, both handmade and ready-to-wear. Fabric from some of the world's leading clothmakers is used in the designs. Linked with Vogini, the famous purveyor of leatherwork, the boutique is a bastion of top-quality craftsmanship and high-fashion style.

La Bottega di Nino. Merceria dell'Orologio, San Marco 223. ☎ **041/5-22-56-08.** Vaporetto: San Marco.

In need of some new threads for the Film Festival? This is the place for elegant male attire. It features the work of many European designers, even some from England, but it shines brightest in its Italian names, such as Nino Cerruti, Valentino, and Zenia. The prices are also better for Italian wear.

Venice Shopping

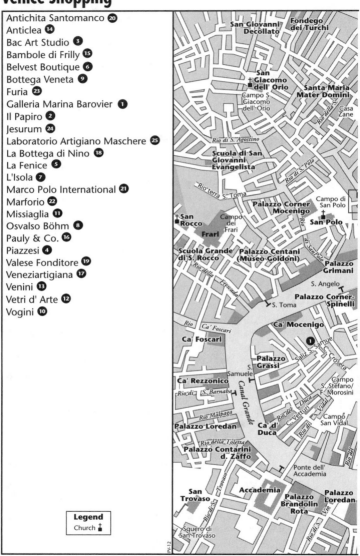

Legend
Church ⛪

San Giovanni Decollato
Fondego dei Turchi
San Giacomo dell' Orio
Santa Maria Mater Domini
Campo S. Giacomo dell'Orio
Casa Zane
Rio di S. Agostino
Scuola di San Giovanni Evangelista
Rio di S. Polo
Rio-terra S.'Toma
Palazzo Corner Mocenigo
Campo di San Polo
San Rocco
Campo dei Frari
San Polo
Frari
Scuola Grande di S. Rocco
Palazzo Centani (Museo Goldoni)
Palazzo Grimani
Rio della Frescada
S. Angelo
S. Toma
Palazzo Corner Spinelli
Rio
Ca' Foscari
Ca' Mocenigo
Ca' Foscari
Calle S. Samue
Crosera
Palazzo Grassi
Samuele
Campo S. Stefano/ F. Morosini
Ca' Rezzonico
Rio di S. Barnaba
Canal Grande
Rio del Duca
C. Vetrin
Campo San Vidal
Rio-Malpaga
Ca' d' Duca
Rio di
Palazzo Loredan
Rio della Toletta
Palazzo Contarini d. Zaffo
Ponte dell' Accademia
Palazzo Loredan
San Trovaso
Trovaso
Accademia
Palazzo Brandolin Rota
Rio di S.
Via
Squero di San Trovaso

142

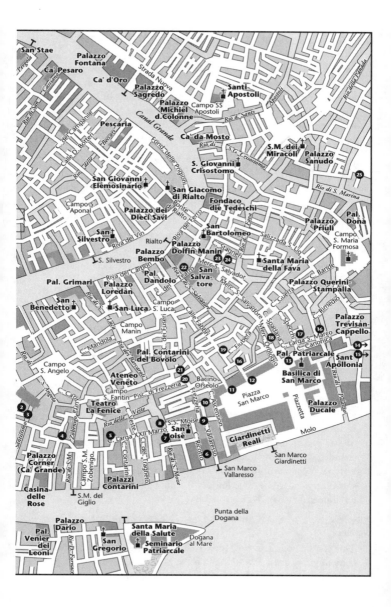

San'Stae
Palazzo Fontana
Ca' Pesaro
Ca' d'Oro
Palazzo Sagredo
Palazzo Michiel d.Colonne
Strada Nuova
Canal Grande
Campo SS Apostoli
Santi Apostoli
Pescaria
Ca' da Mosto
S.M. dei Miracoli
Palazzo Sanudo
S. Giovanni Crisostomo
San Giovanni Elemosinario
San Giacomo di Rialto
Fondaco die Tedeschi
Rio di S. Marina
Campo Aponal
Palazzo dei Dieci Savi
San Bartolomeo
Pal. Donà
Palazzo Priuli
Campo S. Maria Formosa
San Silvestro
Rialto
Palazzo Dolfin-Manin
Santa Maria della Fava
Palazzo Bembo
Palazzo Querini-Stampalia
Pal. Grimani
Palazzo Loredan
Pal. Dandolo
San Salvatore
San Benedetto
San Luca
Campo S. Luca
Palazzo Trevisan-Cappello
Campo Manin
Pal. Contarini del Bovolo
Campo S. Angelo
Pal. Patriarcale
Sant' Apollonia
Ateneo Veneto
Basilica di San Marco
Teatro La Fenice
S.S. Moisè
San Moisè
Piazza San Marco
Palazzo Ducale
Palazzo Corner (Ca' Grande)
Giardinetti Reali
Palazzi Contarini
San Marco Giardinetti
Casina delle Rose
S.M. del Giglio
San Marco Vallaresso
Molo
Palazzo Dario
Santa Maria della Salute
Punta della Dogana
Pal. Venier dei Leoni
San Gregorio
Seminario Patriarcale
Dogana al Mare

143

La Fenice. Calle Larga XXII Marzo, San Marco 2255. ☎ **041/5-23-12-73.** Vaporetto: San Marco.

Despite the similarity of its name with one of Venice's most legendary theaters, this is a large well-stocked outlet for some of Italy's most visible clothing manufacturers. One of four outlets of a citywide chain, La Fenice sells clothing for men and women from designers like Ferré, Dior, Montana, Mosquino, Mügler, and Thierry.

GLASS

Anticlea. Campo San Provolo, Castello 4719. ☎ **041/528-6949.** Vaporetto: San Zaccaria.

Harking back to the days when they were used for trade in Venetian colonies, this shop offers scores of antique and reproduction glass beads, strung or unstrung, in many sizes, shapes, and colors.

Domus. Fondamenta dei Vetrai 82, Murano. ☎ **041/739-215.** Vaporetto: 12 or 13 to Murano.

On the island of Murano, home of the actual glassworks, this shop offers a good selection of designs by the island's top artisans. Prevalent are smaller objects like jewelry, vases, bowls, bottles, and drinking glasses. Here you'll find designs by Carlo Moretti.

✪ **Galleria Marina Barovier.** Salizzada San Samuele, San Marco 3216. ☎ **041/523-6748.** Vaporetto: San Samuele.

Don't come here hoping to find a Murano-style glass trinket similar to the thousands of others sold throughout Venice, as it's the high-glamour repository for some of Italy's most creative modern glass sculptures. Since it was opened in the early 1980s by its namesake, Marina Barovier, in the unlikely Venetian suburb of Mestre, it has grown in stature. Especially sought after are sculptures by master glassmakers Lino Tagliapietra and Dale Chihuly, whose chandeliers represent amusing and/or dramatic departures from traditional Venetian forms. Don't despair if you're on a budget, as some simple items begin as low as 20,000L ($11.60). Anything can be shipped.

L'Isola. Campo San Moisè, San Marco 1468. ☎ **041/523-1973.** Vaporetto: Vallaresso.

This is the shop of Carlo Moretti, one of the world's best-known contemporary artisans working in glass. You'll find all his signature designs in decanters, drinking glasses, vases, bowls, and paperweights.

Marco Polo International s.n.c. Frezzeria, San Marco 1644. ☎ **041/ 522-9295.** Vaporetto: Vallaresso.

Venetian Carnevale Masks

Venetian masks, considered collectors' items, originated during Carnevale, which takes place the week before the beginning of Lent. In the old days there was a good reason to wear masks during the riotous Carnival, as they allowed anonymity to unfaithful wives and husbands and priests breaking their vows of chastity. Things got so out of hand that Carnevale was banned in the late 18th century. But it came back—and the masks went on again.

You can find shops selling masks practically on every corner. As with glass and lace, however, quality varies. Many masks are great artistic expressions; others are shoddy and cheap. The most sought-after mask is the *Portafortuna* (luck bringer), with its long nose and birdlike visage. *Orientale* masks evoke the heyday of the Serene Republic and its trade with the Far East. The *Bauta* was worn by men to assert their macho qualities, and the *Neutra* blends the facial characteristics of both sexes. The list of masks and their origins seems endless.

The best place to buy Carnevale masks is the **Laboratorio Artigiano Maschere,** Barbaria delle Tole, Castello 6657 (☎ **041/ 522-3110**), which sells handcrafted masks in papier-mâché or leather. This well-established store has a particularly good selection, including masks depicting the characters of the commedia dell'arte. The shop also sells a variety of other handcrafted papier-mâché items, like picture and mirror frames, pots, consoles, and boxes in the shape of pets.

Also good is **Mondonovo,** Rio Terrà Canal, Dorsoduro 3063 (☎ **041/528-7344**), where talented artisans produce copies of both traditional and more modern masks, each of which is one-of-a-kind and richly nuanced with references to Venetian lore and traditions. Prices range from 30,000L ($17) for a fairly basic model to 3,000,000L ($1,740) for something you might display on a wall as a piece of sculpture.

Quality Murano glass items fill this 2-story shop. Among the items designed and handblown by the island's artisans are one-of-a-kind sculptures, drinking glasses, boxes, and paperweights. The front display area on the ground floor features small pieces, which, though not cheap, make ideal souvenirs.

✪ **Pauly & Co.** Ponte dei Consorzi, San Marco 4392. ☎ **041/5-20-98-99.** Vaporetto: San Zaccaria.

One of the oldest (founded in 1866) and largest purveyors of traditional Venetian glass is Pauly, whose labyrinth of showrooms—more than two dozen of them—are a highly visible part of Venice's commercial texture. Part of the premises is devoted to something akin to a museum, where past successes (now antiques) are displayed with pride. Antique items are only rarely offered for sale, but they can be copied and shipped to virtually anywhere, and chandeliers can be electrified in accordance with the standards of where you live. Chandeliers begin at about 2,000,000L ($1,160) but frequently spiral to as much as 1,000,000,000L ($580,000) in the case of some Saudi emirs who designed entire throne rooms around them.

✪ **Venini.** Piazzetta Leoncini, San Marco 314. ☎ **041/5-22-40-45.** Vaporetto: San Zaccaria.

Venini's Venetian art glass has caught the attention of collectors from all over the world. Many of their pieces, including anything-but-ordinary lamps, bottles, and vases, are works of art and represent the best of Venetian craftsmanship. Along with the previously recommended Pauly & Co., Venini represents the master craftspeople of Venetian glassmakers. Its best-known glass has a distinctive swirl pattern in several colors, called a *venature*. This shop is known for the refined quality of its glass, some of which appears almost transparent. Much of it's very fragile, but they learned long ago how to ship it anywhere safely. To visit the furnace, call ☎ **041/739-955.**

Vetri d'Arte. Piazza San Marco, San Marco 140. ☎ **041/520-0205.** Vaporetto: Vallaresso.

Here you can find moderately priced glass jewelry for souvenirs and gifts, as well as a selection of pricier crystal jewelry and porcelain bowls.

GRAPHICS

Bac Art Studio. Campo San Maurizio, San Marco 2663. ☎ **041/5-22-81-71.** Vaporetto: Santa Maria del Giglio.

This studio sells paper goods, but it's mainly a graphics gallery, noted for its selection of engravings, posters, and lithographs representing Venice at Carnevale time. Items for the most part are reasonably priced; care and selection obviously went into the gallery's choice of its merchandise.

Osvaldo Böhm. Salizzada San Moisè, San Marco 1349–1350. ☎ **041/5-22-22-55.** Vaporetto: San Marco.

Head here for that just right, and light, souvenir. Osvaldo Böhm has a rich collection of photographic archives specializing in Venetian art as well as original engravings and maps, lithographs, watercolors, and Venetian masks. You can also see modern serigraphs by local artists and some fine handcrafted bronzes.

HANDCRAFTS

Veneziartigiana. Calle Larga, San Marco 412–413. ☎ **041/5-23-50-32.** Vaporetto: San Marco.

This emporium assembles into one showroom the artisanal production of at least 11 local craftspeople, whose creations in silver, glass, ceramics, wood, and copper are a noteworthy improvement over the inventories of some nearby competitors. Look for well-executed dolls, Carnevale masks, picture frames, and posters, all of which would make super gifts for relatives or friends back home.

JEWELRY

✪ **Missiaglia.** Piazza San Marco, San Marco 125. ☎ **041/5-22-44-64.** Vaporetto: San Marco.

Since 1846, Missiaglia has been the private supplier to rich Venetians and savvy shoppers from around the world seeking the best in gold and jewelry. Go here for that special classic piece. But, as the family keeps a sharp watch on the latest developments in international jewelry design, something a little more cutting edge might catch your eye. Their specialty is colored precious and semiprecious gemstones set in white or yellow gold settings.

LACE

✪ **Jesurum.** Merceria del Capitello, San Marco 4857. ☎ **041/5-20-61-77.** Vaporetto: San Zaccaria.

For serious purchases, Jesurum is the best place. This elegant shop, a center of noted lace makers and fashion creators, is located in a 12th-century palazzo. You'll find Venetian handmade or machine-made lace and embroidery on table, bed, and bath linens, plus hand-printed swimsuits. Quality and originality are guaranteed and special orders are accepted. The exclusive linens are expensive, but the inventory is large enough to accommodate any kind of budget. Staff members insist that everything sold is made in or around Venice in traditional patterns, with almost no emphasis on imports from China or other parts of Asia.

LEATHER

Bottega Veneta. Calle Vallaresso, San Marco 1337. ☎ **041/5-20-28-16.** Vaporetto: San Marco.

Bottega Veneta is primarily known for its woven leather bags. These bags are sold elsewhere too, but the prices are less at the company's flagship outlet here. The shop also sells shoes for men and women, suitcases, belts, and everything made of leather. There's also an array of high-fashion accessories.

Furla. Merceria del Capitello, San Marco 4954. ☎ **041/5-23-06-11.** Vaporetto: Rialto.

Furla is a specialist in women's leather bags. It also sells belts and gloves for women. Many of the bags are stamped with molds, making them appear to be alligator, lizard, or some other exotic creature. They come in a varied choice of colors, including what Austrians call "Maria Theresa ochre." Furla also displays a varied selection of costume jewelry and an array of belts, silk scarves, briefcases, and wallets.

✪ **Marforio.** Campo San Salvador, San Marco 5033. ☎ **041/5-22-57-34.** Vaporetto: Rialto.

Marforio is in the heart of the city. Founded in 1875, it's the oldest and largest leather-goods retail outlet in Italy. The company, run by the same family for five generations, is known for the quality of its leather products, and this outlet has an enormous assortment. You'll find all the famous European labels—Valentino, Armani, Cerruti, and Cardin, among others.

Vogini. Calle dell'Ascensione, San Marco 1291, 1292, and 1301 (near Harry's Bar). ☎ **041/5-22-25-73.** Vaporetto: San Marco.

Every kind of leatherwork is offered here, especially women's handbags, which are exclusive models. There are also handbags in petit-point embroideries and crocodile as well as men's and women's shoes. Brand names include Armani, Mosquino, Versace, and products designed and manufactured by Vogini itself. The travel-equipment department contains a large assortment of trunks and both hard- and soft-sided suitcases and makeup cases.

MARKETS

If you're looking for some bargain-basement buys, head not for any basement but to one of the little shops lining the **Rialto Bridge** (Vaporetto: Rialto). You'll find a wide assortment of merchandise, from angora sweaters to leather gloves. Quality is likely to vary widely, so plunge in with the utmost discrimination.

PAPER & STATIONERY

Florence is still the major center in Italy for artistic paper—especially marbleized paper. However, craftspeople in Venice still make marble paper by hand, sheet by sheet. The technique of marbling paper originated in Japan as early as A.D. 1000, spreading through Persia and finally reaching Europe in the 1400s. Except for France, marbling had largely disappeared with the coming of the Industrial Revolution, but it was revived in Venice in the 1970s. Each sheet of handmade marbleized paper is one of a kind.

✪ **Il Papiro.** Campo San Maurizio, San Marco 2764. ☎ **041/5-22-30-55.** Vaporetto: San Maria del Giglio.

If you never considered paper and stationery a high art form, think again, as this upscale purveyor of the raw ingredients needed for elegant correspondence is among the most sought-after in the world. Regardless of your personal literary style, whatever you compose is bound to look better (and make you feel better) if it's recorded on the high-fiber hand-printed pages that are stocked here. Thinking of sending off a handwritten proposal of marriage? Pen it on something from Il Papiro, as it will certainly look a lot more impressive. There's also a full supply of gift items, like photo albums, address books, picture frames, diaries, and boxes covered in artfully printed paper.

✪ **Piazzesi.** Campieillo della Feltrina, San Marco 2511. ☎ **041/5-22-12-02.** Vaporetto: Santa Maria del Giglio.

One of Venice's most stylish shops for paper and writing supplies is Piazzesi, which claims to be the oldest purveyor of writing paper in Italy (opened in 1900). It sells elegant versions of stationery that require as many as 13 artisans to produce. Most of the production here is hand-blocked, marbleized, stenciled, and/or accented with dyes that are blown onto each sheet with a small breath-operated tube. Also look for papier-mâché masks and commedia dell'arte–style statues representing age-old professions like architects, carpenters, doctors, glassmakers, church officials, and notaries. Seeking for something more modern? Consider any of the whimsically decorated containers for CDs and computer diskettes.

9

Venice After Dark

*F*or such a fabled city, Venice's nightlife is pretty meager. Who wants to hit the nightclubs when strolling the city at night is more interesting than any spectacle staged inside? Ducking into a cafe or bar for a brief interlude, however, is a nice way to break up your evening walk. Although it offers gambling and a few other diversions, Venice is pretty much an early-to-bed town. Most restaurants close at midnight.

The best guide to what's happening in Venice is ***Un Ospite di Venezia,*** a free pamphlet (part in English, part in Italian) distributed by the tourist office. It lists any music and opera or theatrical presentations, along with art exhibitions and local special events.

In addition, classical concerts are often featured in various churches, such as the Chiesa di Vivaldi. To see if any **church concerts** are being presented at the time of your visit, call ☎ **041/5-20-87-22** for information.

1 The Performing Arts

In January 1996 a dramatic fire left the fabled La Fenice at Campo San Fantin, the city's main venue for performing arts, a blackened shell and a smoldering ruin. Opera lovers around the world, including Luciano Pavarotti, mourned its loss. The Italian government has pledged $12.5 million for the rebuilding of the theater, once the most beautiful in Italy, but the reconstruction has been mired in controversy. Optimistic predictions suggest that the theater *may* reopen around the millennium.

Despite the tragic loss of Teatro la Fenice, cultural presentations have continued in a less glamorous form in a temporary theater that the city of Venice erected as a short-term substitute. Designed in the form of a big circus-style tent, within walking distance of the Piazzale Roma, it's the **Teatro Temporaneo la Fenice** (also known as **Palafenice**), Isola Tronchetto (☎ **041/521-0161;** vaporetto: Line 1 to Tronchetto). For a list of other cultural performances in Venice, contact either the tourist office or City Hall (Communale Municipio di Venezia; ☎ **041/274-8200**).

This is, after all, the city of Vivaldi, and if you're lucky, you might catch a performance of *The Four Seasons* at the ✪ **Chiesa di Vivaldi** (☎ **041/52-31-096**), officially known as the Chiesa della Pietà. There are Vivaldi performances at other churches, but this church, where the "red priest" (nicknamed because of his red hair, not his politics) was once choral director is the main venue. Tickets are sold at the church's box office on the Riva degli Schiavoni or at the desk of the next door Metropole Hotel, and cost around 40,000L ($23) for adults and 25,000L ($14) for students.

Teatro Goldoni. Calle Goldoni (near Campo San Luca). ☎ **041/5-20-75-83.** Tickets 18,000L–66,000L ($10.45–$38.30). Vaporetto: Rialto.

This theater, close to the Ponte di Rialto in the San Marco district, honors Carlo Goldoni (1707–93), the most prolific—critics say the best—Italian playwright. The theater presents a changing repertoire of productions, often plays in Italian, but musical presentations as well. The box office is open Monday through Saturday from 10am to 1pm and 4:30 to 7pm.

2   The Bar Scene

Want more in the way of nightlife? All right, but be warned: The Venetian bar owners may sock it to you when they present the bill.

Bar ai Speci. In the Hotel Panada, Calle dei Specchieri, San Marco 646. ☎ **041/5-20-90-88.** Vaporetto: San Marco.

The Bar ai Speci is a charming corner bar located only a short walk from St. Mark's Basilica. Its richly grained paneling is offset by dozens of antique mirrors, each different, whose glittering surfaces reflect the rows of champagne and scotch bottles and the clustered groups of Biedermeier chairs.

Bar Ducale. Calle delle Ostreghe, San Marco 2354. ☎ **041/5-21-00-02.** Vaporetto: San Marco.

Bar Ducale occupies a tiny corner of a building near a bridge over a narrow canal. Customers stand at the zinc bar facing the carved 19th-century Gothic-reproduction shelves. Mimosas are the specialty here, but tasty sandwiches are also offered. The ebullient owner learned his craft at Harry's Bar before going into business for himself. Today his small establishment is usually mobbed every day of the week. It's ideal for an early evening apéritif as you stroll about.

Bar Salus. Campo Santa Margherita, Dorsoduro. ☎ **041/528-5279.** Vaporetto: Ca' Rezzonico.

Don't expect the aristocracies of Venice, or a group of monks and

The "Folly & Madnesse" of Carnevale

John Evelyn (1620–1706) is best remembered for his *Diary,* in which he recounted the details of his travels abroad. In 1646, he showed up in Venice at Carnival time, noting its "folly & madnesse." He wasn't always happy with what he saw—especially the "flinging of eggs fill'd with sweete Waters, & sometimes not over sweete; they also have a barbarous costome of hunting bulls about the Streetes & Piazzas, which is very dangerous, the passages being generally so narrow in that Citty."

Revived in 1979, Venice's Carnevale in February is a much tamer affair today, but the memory of its "shameful" past lives on. You too can become part of the fun. All you need do is deck yourself out in plumes and sequins of cosmic fantasy or wear something in which Casanova would've felt right at home.

Be warned: At the peak of Carnival it's almost impossible to pass through Piazza San Marco and its narrow neighboring streets. You can bring masks and costumes from home or purchase them here from the various well-stocked mask and costume stores (see the box "Venetian Carnevale Masks" in chapter 8). Of course, bring a camera and lots of film. Naturally you'll want to purchase concert tickets the moment you arrive to ensure yourself a seat.

Today's pre-Lenten celebration is an offshoot of the Carnevale from the heyday of Le Serenissima in the 1700s. (Actually, Carnevale was founded in 1094.) Men and women with a roving eye traveled across Europe to partake of the debauchery and the thrill of the celebration. The wearing of masks began as a tradition allowing nobles to mingle incognito with ordinary Venetians in the casini and theaters. Thus, the masked aristocratic lady could

nuns, at this rough-and-ready bar near Ca' Rezzonico. A shot of whisky or a beer at the long stand-up bar offers insight into the sometimes raucous nuts and bolts that keep the city more or less intact. There's no music, and it seems to be a rendezvous for clients who appear to have known each another since the days of the Doges.

Devil's Forest. Calle Stagneri, San Marco 5185. ☎ **041/520-0623.** Vaporetto: Rialto.

fulfill her fantasies and end up making love to a gondolier and he'd never know her true identity.

The classic mask is the angular white beaklike form extending over the chin (a *bauto*), as depicted in genre scenes painted by Pietro Longhi. There are variations of this. One is made up of a black silk hood and a delicate lace cape that's then covered by a voluminous cloak (*tabarro*). When a three-corner hat is placed over the head, with a mask covering most of the face, a merrymaker can travel almost anywhere without being recognized.

One 18th-century Venetian woman wrote, "Even my own husband didn't know me when I spotted him engaged with another woman. Of course, I forgave him and never mentioned his indiscretion, less he learn of my own. After all, it was Carnevale!"

Nowadays masks are worn more for the sake of cutting a dash or posing for the paparazzi than they are to cover major indiscretions. Sometimes costumes are coordinated into groups. The most original we've ever seen was a group that came dressed as *The Banquet of the House of Levi* by Veronese.

Carnevale opens with a series of lavish balls and private parties, though there's still plenty of fun in the streets if you don't get a major invitation. The merrymakers carry on until Shrove Tuesday, when the bells of San Francesco della Vigna toll at midnight. But before they do, the grand finale involves fireworks over the lagoon. There's a lighthearted feel to this otherwise introverted and rather insular city. Nowhere in Europe will you likely see as many people carousing, dancing, drinking, and playing games of flirtation.

At Carnevale time, Venice becomes more Hollywood in character than ever—no wonder it was Walt Disney's favorite city.

Set within a stone's throw from the Rialto Bridge, this is an authentic Irish pub where long-term clients have reached a comfortable balance between the English- and Italian-speaking worlds. You'll find a comfortingly predictable roster of beers and ales on tap here (Guinness, Harp, Kilkenny, and a line of German beers), lots of references to European travel by the well-versed clients, and platters of food that average between 8,000L and 12,000L ($4.65 and $6.95). Don't expect bangers and mash, as things are more Mediterranean than that, with lots of emphasis on sandwiches, pastas, and simple grills.

Do Leoni. In the Londra Palace Hotel, Riva degli Schiavoni, Castello 4171. ☎ **041/5-20-05-33.** Vaporetto: San Zaccaria.

The hotel's exclusive restaurant has already been recommended (see chapter 5, "Dining"). Here, the interior is a rich blend of scarlet-and-gold carpeting with a lion motif, English pub-style furniture, and Louis XVI–style chairs, along with plenty of exposed mahogany. While sipping your cocktail, you'll enjoy a view of a 19th-century bronze statue, the lagoon, and the foot traffic along the Grand Canal.

Fiddler's Elbow. Corte dei Pali, Cannaregio 3847. ☎ **041/5-23-99-30.** Vaporetto: Ca' d'Oro.

Five minutes from the Rialto Bridge in the Cannaregio district, this pub—called an Irish pub by the Venetians—is run by the same people who operate equally popular Fiddler's Elbows in both Florence and Rome. Since its opening late in 1992, it has become one of Venice's most popular watering holes. They have the only satellite TV in Venice with all the channels—Sky, American, Sports, Music, whatever. In the summer, there is live outdoor music.

Guanotto. Ponte del Lovo, 4819. ☎ **041/5-20-84-39.** Vaporetto: Rialto.

From bustling premises one floor above street level, this bar and cafe has attracted clients from throughout the neighborhood since it was established in 1884. Within either of two old-fashioned rooms, you can order such drinks as whisky, an array of coffees, hot chocolate, and a house specialty (spritz) that combines white wine with seltzer waters and bitters. Toast, pastries, and ice cream are the only food served. Except during busy days in midsummer, many visitors find it a bit more soothing, and less frenetic, than many of the ground-floor cafes nearby.

✪ **Harry's Bar.** Calle Vallaresso, San Marco 1323. ☎ **041/5-28-57-77.** Vaporetto: San Marco.

The single most famous of all Ernest Hemingway's watering holes, Harry's Bar is known for inventing its own drinks and exporting them around the world. It's also said that carpaccio, the delicate raw-beef dish, was invented here. Fans say that Harry's makes the best Bellini in the world. A libation costs 16,000L ($10.25), although many old-time visitors still prefer a vodka martini at 12,000L ($7.70). Harry's Bar is found around the world, from Munich to Los Angeles, from Paris to Rome, but this is the original. Except for a restaurant, Harry Cipriani in New York City, the other bars are unauthorized knockoffs. In Venice, the bar is a Venetian tradition and landmark—not quite as famous as the Basilica di San Marco, but almost. Celebrities frequent the place during the various film and art festivals.

Martini Scala Club. Campo San Fantin, San Marco 1980. ☎ **041/ 5-22-41-21.** Vaporetto: San Marco or Santa Maria del Giglio.

Martini Scala Club is an elegant restaurant with a piano bar. It has functioned as some kind of inn in one manifestation or another since 1724. You can enjoy its food and wine until 2am—it's the only kitchen in Venice that stays open late. Dishes include smoked goose breast with grapefruit and arugula, fresh salmon with black butter and olives, and gnocchi (dumplings) with butter and sage. The piano bar gets going after 10pm. It's possible to order drinks without having food.

Paradiso Perduto. Fondamenta della Misericordia, Cannaregio 2540. ☎ **041/720-581.** Vaporetto: San Marcuola.

Early every evening except Wednesday, this authentic hostaria functions as a likable tavern, serving well-prepared platters of seafood to locals who live close to Venice's train station, far from the touristic congestion around St. Mark's Square. If you're interested in dining (the frittura mista of fish, served with polenta, is wonderful), main courses range from 8,000L to 25,000L ($4.65 to $14.50), and are served Thursday to Tuesday from 7 to 10:30pm. But the real heart and soul of the place is the time after 11pm, when a mixture of soft recorded music and live piano music creates a backdrop for conversation until at least 2am.

3 Wine Bars

Cantina do Spade. Calle do Spade, San Polo 860. ☎ **041/5-21-05-74.** Vaporetto: Rialto.

This historic wine bar beneath an arcade near the main fish and fruit market dates from 1475. It was once a hangout of Casanova's. Venetians call it a *bacaro* instead of a wine bar. The place is completely rustic and bare bones, but devotees come here to order *cicchetti* (equivalent to Spanish tapas), of which there are 250 varieties. Often in-season game dishes, including boar, deer, and reindeer, are served, but don't count on this. Venetians delight in the 220 different wines, beginning at 1,500L ($.85) per glass. The place is a local favorite, and has been for centuries, but don't come here looking for glamour; head for Harry's Bar if that's what you're after.

Mascareta. Calle Lunga Santa Maria Formosa, Castello 5138. ☎ **041/ 5-23-07-44.** Vaporetto: Rialto.

This wine bar was established in 1995. The focus is on Italian wines, many from the Veneto region, which are priced at 2,000L ($1.15) a glass, depending on the vintage. There's only room for 20 people, seated at cramped tables in an old Venetian building, but if you're hungry you can order simple platters of snack-style food (prosciutto, cheese plates, and other dishes) priced at 12,000L to 18,000L ($6.95 to $10.45), depending on what's available that day.

✪ **Vino Vino.** Ponte della Veste, San Marco 2007. ☎ **041/5-23-70-27.** Vaporetto: San Marco.

You can choose from more than 250 Italian and imported wines here. Vino Vino attracts a varied clientele: It wouldn't be unusual to see a Venetian countess sipping Prosecco near a gondolier eating a meal. This place is loved by everyone from snobs to young people to almost-broke visitors. It offers wines by the bottle or glass, including Italian grappas. Popular Venetian dishes are also served, including pastas, beans, baccalà (codfish), and polenta. The two rooms are always jammed like a vaporetto at rush hour, and there's take-away service if you can't find a place.

4 The Cafe Scene

Caffè Chioggia. Piazza San Marco, 11. ☎ **041/5-28-50-11.** Vaporetto: San Marco.

Although it isn't the only cafe whose entrance opens onto the Piazza San Marco, it's the only one with a view of the Venetian lagoon (off to one side), and the only one offering live music that continues in one form or another throughout the day and evening. Starting around 10am and continuing, with reasonable breaks, until 1:30am, piano bar music might begin the day, eventually terminating with a jazz trio. Chioggia has been flourishing here since the 1930s. Don't expect a full-fledged restaurant, as the only food items served include light platters and sandwiches. Drinks include whisky with soda, beer, and endless cups of coffee.

✪ **Caffè Florian.** Piazza San Marco, San Marco 56–59. ☎ **041/5-28-53-38.** Vaporetto: San Marco.

This is Venice's most famous cafe. The Florian was built in 1720, and it remains romantic and elegant—a pure Venetian salon with red plush banquettes, intricate murals under glass, and art nouveau lighting and lamps. It's the most fashionable and aristocratic rendezvous in Venice. The Florian roster of customers in the distant past has included Casanova, Lord Byron, Goethe, Canova, de Musset, and Madame de Staël. Light lunch is served from noon to 3pm, costing 20,000L ($11.60) and up, and an English tea from 3 to 6pm, when you can select from a choice of pastries, ice cream, and cakes. An espresso is 6,000L ($3.50); long drinks cost 19,000L ($11), plus 5,000L ($2.90) extra if you drink on the square when music is playing (April through October only).

Gran Caffè Lavena. Piazza San Marco, San Marco 133–134. ☎ **041/ 5-22-40-70.** Vaporetto: San Marco.

This popular but intimate cafe under the arcades of Piazza San Marco was once frequented by Richard Wagner when he stayed in Venice. It has some of the most beautifully ornate glass chandeliers in the city—the kind you'll love even if you hate Venetian glass. They hang from the ceiling between the iron rails of an upper-level balcony. The most interesting tables are near the plate-glass window in front, although there's plenty of room at the stand-up bar as well. Coffee costs 1,500L (85¢) if you're standing, 5,500L ($3.20) if you're sitting at a table. And there's a music surcharge of 5,000L ($2.90).

✪ **Quadri.** Piazza San Marco, San Marco 120–124. ☎ **041/5-28-92-99.** Vaporetto: San Marco.

Quadri, recommended in chapter 5 as a restaurant, stands on the opposite side of the square from the Florian. It, too, is elegantly decorated in antique style. It should be—it was founded in 1638. Wagner used to drop in for a drink when he was in Venice working on *Tristan and Isolde*. Its prices are virtually the same as at the Florian, and it, too, imposes a surcharge on drinks ordered during concert periods. The bar was a favorite with the Austrians during their long-ago occupation (Venetian patriots went to Florian's). A whisky costs 17,000L ($9.85); coffee 5,500L ($3.20). The music surcharge is 4,000L ($2.30).

5 Ice Cream & Pastries

Gelateria Paolin. Campo San Stefano, San Marco 2962A. ☎ **041/ 5-22-55-76.** Vaporetto: Santa Maria del Giglio.

For many, strolling to the Gelateria Paolin (set in a large colorful square) and ordering some of the tastiest ice cream (gelato) in Venice is nightlife enough. That's the way many a Venetian spends a summer evening. This gelateria has stood on the corner of this busy square since the 1930s, making it the oldest ice cream parlor in Venice. You can order your ice cream to eat at one of the sidewalk tables (which costs more) or order it to go. Many interesting flavors are offered. Your best bet is one of the ice creams made with fresh fruit from the Veneto.

Pasticceria Marchini. Campo San Maurizio, San Marco 2769. ☎ **041/5-22-91-09.** Vaporetto: Accademia.

If you'd like to escape the throngs of visitors that overrun Venice in the early evening, head here, have a pastry and a coffee, and contemplate your evening plans. This is where your Venetian friend (if you have one) would take you for the most delectable pastries served in the city. The small pastries are made according to old recipes—ask for their bigna or cannolo.

6   A Dance Club

Il Piccolo Mondo. Calle Contarini Corfu 1056A. ☎ **041/520-0371.** Cover (including the 1st drink) 12,000L ($6.95) Thurs–Fri, 18,000L ($10.45) Sat; otherwise free. Vaporetto: Accademia.

This pub, near the Accademia, is open during the day, and at night it features disco dancing and organized parties. The crowd is often young, and dance music prevails. It's open from Thursday to Tuesday from 10pm to 4am, but the action actually doesn't begin until after midnight.

7   Casinos

Casino Municipale. Lungomare G. Marconi 4, Lido di Venezia. ☎ **041/5-29-71-11.** Admission 18,000L ($10.45). Vaporetto: Casino Express.

If you want to risk your luck and your lire, take a vaporetto ride on the Casino Express, which leaves from stops at the railway station, Piazzale Roma, and Piazzetta San Marco, and delivers you to the landing dock of the Casino Municipale. The Italian government forbids its nationals to cross the threshold unless they work here, so bring your passport. The building itself is foreboding, almost as if it could have been inspired by Mussolini-era architects. However, the action gets hotter once you step inside. You can try your luck at blackjack, roulette, baccarat, or whatever. You can also dine, drink at the bar, or enjoy a floor show. Open June to September daily 4pm to 2:30am.

Vendramin-Calergi Palace. Strada Nuova, Cannaregio 2040. ☎ **041/5-29-71-11.** Admission 18,000L ($10.45). Vaporetto: San Marcuola.

From October through May, the casino action moves to the Vendramin-Calergi Palace. Incidentally, in 1883 Wagner died in this house, which opens onto the Grand Canal. Open daily 3pm to 2:30am.

10

Side Trips from Venice

Venice's islands are easily reached by vaporetto. Murano, the island of glassmaking, is interesting and is the most popular side trip, but it's not the most beautiful of the nearby islands. Both Burano and Torcello are more attractive.

1 Murano

This is the island where for centuries **glassblowers** have turned out those fantastic chandeliers that Victorian ladies used to prize so highly. They also produce heavily ornamented glasses so ruby-red or so indigo-blue you can't tell if you're drinking blackberry juice or pure grain alcohol. Happily, the glassblowers are still plying their trade, although increasing competition—notably from Sweden—has compelled a greater degree of sophistication in design.

You can combine a tour of Murano with a trip along the lagoon. To reach it, take vaporetto no. 52 from Riva degli Schiavoni, a short walk from Piazzetta San Marco. The boat docks at the landing platform at Murano where—lo and behold—the first furnace conveniently awaits. It's best to go Monday to Friday from 10am to noon if you want to see some glassblowing action. You can also take an organized tour of the three islands (see chapter 6, section 7) but it is easy to go on your own.

THE GLASS FACTORIES & OTHER SIGHTS

As you stroll through Murano, you'll find that the factory owners are only too glad to let you come in and see them ply their age-old craft. These managers aren't altogether altruistic, of course. While browsing through the showrooms, you'll need stiff resistance to keep the salespeople at bay. And it's possible to bargain down the initial price quoted. Don't—repeat *don't*—pay the marked price on any item. That's merely the figure at which to open negotiations.

What's not negotiable is the price of made-on-the-spot souvenirs. For example, you might want to purchase a horse streaked with blue. The artisan takes a piece of incandescent glass, huffs, puffs, rolls it, shapes it, snips it, and behold—he has shaped a horse. The showrooms of Murano also contain a fine assortment of Venetian crystal beads, available in every hue of the rainbow. You may find some of the most appealing work to be the experiments of apprentices.

While on the island, you can visit the Renaissance palazzo that houses the glass museum, the **Museo Vetrario di Murano** on Fondamenta Giustinian (☎ 041/73-95-86), which showcases a spectacular collection of Venetian glass through the centuries. A visit here will put age-old legacy into perspective, and is recommended for those who intend to make a major purchase. It's open Monday, Tuesday, and Thursday through Saturday from 10am to 5pm April through October, and from 10am to 4pm November through March. Admission is 8,000L ($4.65) for adults and 5,000L ($2.90) for children.

If you're looking for a respite from the glass factories, head to the **Church of San Pietro Martire,** Fondamenta Vetrai (☎ 041/73-97-04), which dates from the 1300s but was rebuilt in 1511 and is richly decorated with paintings by Tintoretto and Veronese. Its proud possession is a *Madonna and Child Enthroned* by Giovanni Bellini, plus two superb altarpieces by the same master. The church is right before the junction with Murano's Grand Canal, about 250 yards from the vaporetto landing stage. It's open daily from 9am to noon and 3 to 6pm; closed for Mass Sunday morning.

Even more notable is **Santi Maria e Donato,** Campo San Donato (☎ 041/73-90-56), which is open daily from 9am to noon and 4 to 6pm, with time variations for Sunday Mass. This building is a stellar example of the Venetian Byzantine style, in spite of its 19th-century restoration. It dates from the 7th century but was reconstructed in the 1100s. The interior is known for its mosaic floor—a parade of peacocks and eagles, as well as other creatures—and a 15th-century ship's-keel ceiling. Over the apse is an outstanding mosaic of the Virgin against a gold background, which dates from the early 1200s.

A STOP AT SAN MICHELE

On your way to Murano, you can stop off for a look at the cemetery island of San Michele. Celebrities buried here include impresario

Keeping the Secret

In the 16th century, any master glassblower escaping Murano with the secrets of the trade was tracked down by the Venetian Republic; as punishment, his hands were cut off or he was murdered.

Serge Diaghilev (1872–1929), who introduced Western Europe to Russian ballet, and composer Igor Stravinsky (1882–1971). Ezra Pound's grave is also here. One of the most influential poets of the 20th century, he was a supporter of Mussolini who remained in Italy during World War II. After the war, he was confined for a time in psychiatric hospitals in lieu of being sent to prison for treason; when he was released, he spent the rest of his life in Italy.

Also on the island is the 15th-century **Church of San Michele,** with its handsome white classical facade and richly decorated interior. It was the first church in Venice to be built in the Renaissance style.

WHERE TO DINE

Ai Vetrai. Fondamenta Manin 29, Murano. ☎ **041/73-92-93.** Reservations recommended. Main courses 17,000L–30,000L ($9.85–$17.40). AE, DC, MC, V. Fri–Wed 1–4pm. Closed Dec 15–Jan 5. Vaporetto: 52 from Central Venice. VENETIAN.

Ai Vetrai entertains and nourishes its guests in a large room not far from the Canale dei Vetrai. If you're looking for fish prepared in the local style, this is it. Most varieties of crustaceans and gilled creatures are available on the spot. However, if you phone ahead and order food for a large party, as the Venetians sometimes do, the owners will prepare what they call "a noble fish." You might begin with a delectable spaghetti in a green clam sauce.

Al Corallo. Fondamenta dei Vetrai 73, Murano. ☎ **041/73-90-80.** Main courses 15,000L–25,000L ($8.70–$14.50); fixed-price menu 18,000L ($10.45). AE, DC, MC, V. Wed–Mon noon–3pm and 7–10pm. Closed mid-Dec to mid-Jan (dates vary). Vaporetto: 52 from Central Venice. VENETIAN.

Small and intimate, and somewhat isolated from the bustle and hurry, this family-run restaurant is one of the best established of the restaurants on the island of Murano. Very little English is spoken, but the place is usually filled with a wide variety of clients from all walks of life. The specialties are typically Venetian, and the service is polite. Locals, many of them workers at the nearby glass factories, choose this place for a well-deserved meal after a morning of hard physical labor, and blend with the tourists. The menu changes daily, according to whatever's available in the local markets, but the fresh grilled fish is always reliable.

2 Burano

Burano became world famous as a center of **lace making,** a craft that reached its pinnacle in the 18th century. The craft may have begun with the wives of fishers, who kept themselves busy while waiting for their husbands to return from the sea. The visitor who can spare a morning to visit this island will be rewarded with a charming little fishing village far removed in spirit from the grandeur of Venice, but only half an hour away by ferry. Boats leave from Fondamenta Nuova on Murano. To reach Fondamenta Nuova, take vaporetto no. 12 or 52 from Riva degli Schiavoni.

EXPLORING THE ISLAND

Once on Burano, you'll discover that the houses of the islanders come in varied colors—sienna, robin's-egg or cobalt blue, barn-red, butterscotch, grass green. If you need a focal point for your excursion, it should be the **Scuola di Merletti di Burano (Museo del Merletto),** S. Martino Destra 183, Burano (☎ **041/73-00-34**), in the center of the fishing village at Piazza Baldassare Galuppi. The museum is open November to March Wednesday to Monday from 10am to 4pm and April to October Wednesday to Monday 10am to 5pm. Admission is 5,000L ($2.90), 3,000L ($1.75) students 6 to 12, free for 5 and under. The Burano School of Lacemaking was founded in 1872 as part of a movement aimed at restoring the age-old craft that had earlier declined, giving way to such other lacemaking centers as Chantilly and Bruges. Go up to the second floor where you can see the lace makers, mostly young women, at their painstaking work and can purchase hand-embroidered or handmade lace items.

After visiting the lace school, walk across the square to the **Duomo** and its leaning campanile (inside, look for the *Crucifixion* by Tiepolo). However, do so at once, because the bell tower is leaning so precariously it looks as if it may topple at any moment.

WHERE TO DINE

Ostaria ai Pescatori. Piazza Baldassare Galuppi 371, Burano. ☎ **041/73-06-50.** Reservations recommended. Main courses 22,000L–30,000L ($12.75–$17.40). AE, MC, V. Thurs–Tues noon–3pm and 6–9:30pm. Closed Dec 25–Jan 25. Vaporetto: 12 or 52. SEAFOOD.

The family that pools its efforts to run this well-known restaurant maintains strong friendships with the local fishers, who often reserve the best parts of their daily catch for preparation in the kitchen here. The cooking is performed by the matriarch of an extended family. The place has gained a reputation as the preserver of a type of simple and unpretentious restaurant unique to Burano. In the local dialect, it's a *buranello*. Clients often take the vaporetto from other sections of Venice (the restaurant lies close to the boat landing) to eat at the plain wooden tables set up either indoors or on the small square in front. Specialties feature all the staples of the Venetian seaside diet, including fish soup, risotto di pesce, pasta seafarer's style, tagliolini in squid ink, and a wide range of crustaceans, plus grilled, fried, and baked fish. Dishes prepared with local game are also available, but you must request them well in advance. Your meal might also include a bottle of the fruity wine from the region.

Trattoria de Romano. Via Baldassare Galuppi 223, Burano. ☎ **041/ 73-00-30.** Reservations recommended. Main courses 18,000L–25,000L ($10.45–$14.50). AE, MC, V. Wed–Mon noon–3pm and 7–9pm. Closed Dec 15–Jan 31. Vaporetto: 12 or 52. VENETIAN.

If you're on the island at mealtime, you may want to join a long line of people who enjoy this rather simple-looking caratteristico, Trattoria de Romano, which is around the corner from the lace school. Founded in 1920 by the Nono family, its grandchildren continue to manage it today. You can enjoy a superb dinner here, which might consist of risotto di pesce (the Italian version of the Valencian paella), followed by fritto misto di pesce, a mixed fish fry from the Adriatic, with savory bits of mullet, squid, and shrimp or risotto nero de seppia (risotto flavored with squid ink).

3 Torcello

Of all the islands of the lagoon, Torcello—the so-called Mother of Venice—offers the most charm. If Burano is behind the times, Torcello is positively antediluvian. You can follow in the footsteps of Hemingway and stroll across a grassy meadow, traverse an ancient stone bridge, and step back into that time when the Venetians first fled from invading barbarians to create a city of Neptune in the lagoon.

To reach Torcello, take vaporetto no. 12 or 14. The trip takes about 45 minutes.

Warning: If you go on your own, don't listen to the savvy gondoliers who hover at the ferry quay. They'll tell you that both the cathedral and the locanda are miles away. Actually, they're both reached after a leisurely 12- to 15-minute stroll along the canal.

EXPLORING THE ISLAND

Torcello has two major attractions: a church with Byzantine mosaics good enough to make Empress Theodora at Ravenna turn as purple with envy as her robe, and a *locanda* (inn) that converts daytrippers into inebriated angels of praise. First the spiritual nourishment before the alcoholic sustenance.

Cattedrale di Torcello, also called the Church of Santa Maria Assunta Isola di Torcello (☎ **041/73-00-84**), is the oldest church in Venice, founded in A.D. 639 and subsequently rebuilt. It stands in a lonely, grassy meadow beside a campanile that dates from the 11th century. It's visited chiefly because of its Byzantine mosaics, rivaling those in St. Mark's. Clutching her child, the weeping Madonna in the apse is a magnificent sight. On the opposite wall is a powerful *Last Judgment.* Byzantine artisans, it seems, were at their best in portraying hell and damnation, and at Santa Maria Assunta they don't disappoint. In their Inferno they have re-created a virtual human stew with the fires stirred by wicked demons. Reptiles slide in and out of the skulls of cannibalized sinners. Open April through October, daily from 10am to 12:30pm and 2:30 to 6:30pm; November through March, daily from 10am to 12:30pm and 2:30 to 5pm. Admission is 1,500L (85¢).

Also of interest is the adjacent church, dedicated to St. Fosca, and a small archaeological museum. The church's hours are the same as the cathedral's, and the museum is open Tuesday to Sunday from 10am to 12:30pm and 2 to 5:30pm; admission is 3,000L ($1.70).

WHERE TO DINE

✪ **Locanda Cipriani.** Piazza S. Fosca 29, Torcello. ☎ **041/73-01-50.** Reservations recommended. Main courses 30,000L–40,000L ($17.40–$23.20). AE, DC, MC, V. Wed–Mon noon–3pm and 7–10pm. Closed Jan 15–Feb 15. Vaporetto: 12 or 14 to Torcello. VENETIAN.

Beloved by Hemingway, the Locanda Cipriani, located just across from the church, is an inn extraordinaire. The term *locanda* usually denotes an inexpensive lodging, rated under the lowliest pensione. However, that's not the case at the Cipriani. This country inn is well appointed, with an open-air dining loggia. The chef features a number of high-priced but savory dishes—in fact, the best food served at any restaurant on the islands of the lagoon. Specialties include cannelloni, a savory fish soup, and a rice pilaf. For an appetizer, try the gnocchi, a Roman-inspired dish made with a semolina base. Most guests prefer the fresh fish from the Adriatic, which can be grilled to your specifications.

Index

See also separate Accommodations and Restaurants index, below.
Page numbers in italics refer to maps.

ACCOMMODATIONS